TORCH IN THE DARK

ONE WOMAN'S JOURNEY

&

JOAN CARLYLE

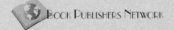

BOOK PUBLISHERS NETWORK

Book Publishers Network
P.O. Box 2256
Bothell • WA • 98041
Pₕ • 425-483-3040
www.bookpublishersnetwork.com

10 9 8 7 6 5 4 3 2 1

Printed in the United States of America

LCCN   2012931049
ISBN   978-1-937454-23-4

Editor: Julie Scandora
Cover Designer: Laura Zugzda
Typographer: Stephanie Martindale

Author's Note

This work is a memoir based on the personal recollections and perceptions of the author. All dialogue is reconstructed from memory. Some names have been changed or omitted.

What would happen if one woman told the truth about her life?
The world would split open.

—Muriel Rukeyser

FOR REUVEN,

And the Carlyle family ... Wendy, Adi, Liat, Zev, and Nava

with love

Contents

g

PART 1

§

BREAKING OPEN

Salem, Oregon. Dammash State Mental Hospital. March 1965. I'm sitting at a table in a corner of the dining room. Mealtimes are trying for me. I hold the fork, but the food won't reach my mouth—food, fork, mouth. I can't make the connection.

Two policewomen enter the large room. The room, filled with babbling patients and staff, becomes quiet, real quiet. The policewomen start walking in my direction. I don't move. I know. I know they are coming for me. One policewoman reaches for my hands. I don't resist. I am handcuffed.

HELP, I NEED SOMEBODY

§

New York. East Village, 1964. We sit in a dark corner of Steve's coffee shop on East Tenth Street.

"Call her," Caty says.

"Call her," Nancy says.

"Go to Portland. She'll help you," Caty says.

Portland, Oregon. It's far away.

Far away from the Lower East Side.

"You can always come back. Go. Renee studied with Bruno Bettelheim. She'll know what to do. We all lived with her at one time or another, Nancy, Ed, Steve, and me. Go."

I call Renee.

"Tom will pick you up."

Will she really help me?

Will she save me from another mental hospital?

My German psychiatrist wants me to go to Hillsdale Hospital.

I won't survive.

Portland. I'm going to Portland.

I pack up my stuff, my knit suits.

I quit my job.

Take my savings, about two thousand dollars. I take it with me in traveler's checks.

In Portland, Tom picks me up.

He is tall, has a beard, wears wire-rim glasses

Tom shakes my hand and says, "How was the trip?"

We get in the truck and drive.

It's too quiet.

He stops in front of a big Victorian wooden house. He carries my bags. Puts them down in the entrance. We walk down a long dark hallway. He opens the door. The light comes in, bright lights. I see light from the wood stove. We are in a big kitchen.

Renee. I see her. She's sitting on a mattress on the floor, plucking on an autoharp. Caty told me Renee was fifty-four; Tom is about my age, thirty years younger than she is. I see long strands of stringy graying hair. She's in a muumuu dress, sitting cross-legged. Her skirt is above her knees. No underpants. I can see everything. I just stare. She doesn't say a word to me. No hello, no how was your trip. She doesn't even look at me, just sits there on the mattress on the kitchen floor, next to the wood stove, playing an autoharp, playing "Oh, freedom. Before I'll be a slave, I'll be buried in my grave …"

I stand there. Pots and pans hanging from the ceiling. Kitchen crammed with coats, cups, bowls, books, bed clothes, silk throws, art supplies, and stuff. Autoharps, there are autoharps all around. On the wall, on the bed, on the chairs.

"Don't just stand there like a fool; take your coat off," Renee shrieks. She keeps strumming away. She stops to sip from a teacup by her side.

"What are you staring at?" she shouts. "What are you doing here, anyway?"

I start to tell her that Caty and Nancy said I should come … but I don't get it out.

"Oh, you're listening to Caty, are you? Well, she went running off with Steve. So what are you going to do?"

What am I going to do? What am I going to do? I thought she would tell me.

The door opens. A guy with blond, curly hair walks across the room. Cute. "I'm Greg." He turns away before I can say hi. He sits down near Renee, picks up a guitar and starts playing. A young, very pretty woman comes in. It must be Sheila, Renee's adopted daughter. Long brown hair, cinched waist, long legs. Me, I'm holding my stomach, my fat stomach. She says, "Hi," and walks across the room to sit on the floor.

"Okay, enough of the show," Renee snorts. "Let her be." Greg hangs around for a while, Sheila leaves. Renee strums some more on the autoharp. The wood stove is cooking away. It's hot. I just stand waiting and waiting and waiting for something to happen.

Renee puts the autoharp down. "Sit down," she orders. "Open up your bags. Now."

I obey. What is she going to do?

"Let me see what you've got there."

One by one, she holds each piece in the air. My carefully packed blue knit suits.

"What are these?"

"My knit suits. I'm a social worker."

Piece by piece, she takes the neatly folded clothing and crumples each one into a ball.

"Here," she says, handing me a scrunched-up knit skirt. "Wash the walls. Now."

It's late. I've flown all the way cross-country. "I'm tired. I'd like to go to bed."

"Bed?" she bellows. "You think you've come all this way to go to bed? No. You're going to wash the walls." She turns to Tom. "Get her a bucket of water."

All in a row, she lays out the crumpled balls of my knit suits.

She dumps the first rolled-up skirt into the soapy water.

"Over here." She wipes the wall with my skirt. "Now you do it." I try.

"No," she yells. "No! You're not doing it right."

She takes the wad from my hand and starts singing as she wipes the wall. She hands me a soapy, rolled-up knit skirt.

"Here you do it." Every time I try, she pulls it out of my hand and says, "No, like this."

She crumples up my skirts; she crumples up the one piece of life I cling to. Late night becomes early morning. Light seeps in the window. I can barely stay on my feet. "I need to sleep," I whimper. Renee bellows back. "You're not going to sleep. Got that? Keep scrubbing." I scrub and scrub as the morning light comes in. "I'm going to bed," Renee announces suddenly. "Tom, take her upstairs."

The bedroom smells musty. The mattress on the floor smells musty. Empty crates on the floor and an old stove and fridge to the side. The bedroom opens to a small bathroom with an old, scuffed linoleum floor.

Tom goes to the hall and gets me a ragged sheet, towel, pillow, and blanket. "That should do it for now," he says. "See you tomorrow. You'll get used to it here."

I stand in the room upstairs, clutching the pillow and blanket. What does he mean tomorrow? It's morning already. Why did I come here? Why did she do that to my knit suits? All night scrubbing walls—that woman is crazy. Caty and Nancy said she was a therapist and she'd save my life, but she's crazier than I am. What will she do to me next? What, what, what?

I'm freezing. *Please, God, get me out of here. Please. I'll be good.* I wash my face in the cold water from the bathroom and get into bed. The thin blanket is useless. It's too cold to sleep. I turn on the gas stove. I want to be warm. I lie down. My head spins. I want to go home, but where is home?

℅

Later—how much later I don't know—footsteps pound up the stairs. The door flies open. Tom stomps over to the stove and shuts it off. "Smells like gas all over the house. This stove doesn't work right. You shouldn't have put it on."

"Get down here." Renee yells from downstairs. "Now!"

I go down. Renee is pacing in the kitchen. She's totally naked. I stare.

"What's the matter with you, leaving the stove on? What were you thinking? You could have killed us all. Don't you ever pull a stunt like that again."

I want to say I was cold, that I don't remember leaving the gas on, but all I can do is stare at this big naked woman with huge sagging breasts. "Sit down," she says. There are no chairs. She points to the edge of her mattress. I sit. Tom's there. Greg walks in. He gets a guitar that's leaning against the wall and starts to strum. He plays an old Wobbly song, maybe "Old Joe." Then he looks at me.

"Are you pregnant?" he asks.

Pregnant? I shake my head no. I hold my stomach. Something inside of me feels pregnant all the time, but what is he talking about? Do I look that awful? Oh, God.

Renee starts again. "You're going to mop this floor," she shrieks. In the middle of the room are a big mop and a big pail full of water. The kind a school janitor uses. My father had one in his store.

Renee dunks the mop into the pail and runs it through the wringer. She holds it out to me and says, "Here, get going."

I take a few swipes at the floor. She grabs the mop back. "No, you idiot, not like that. See, learn how to do it!"

"But I am a social worker!"

She laughs. "Wash the floors!"

Every time I do a part of the floor, she screams at me. "No, not like that. Do it right!" I'm trying. I want to do it right. I want to do something right.

COMING OF AGE IN A MENTAL HOSPITAL

&

New York, 1962. Twenty-one years old. Evie and I live across the hall from each other at Douglass College, Rutgers University. She talks about how the world should be—her anger, my anger—the injustice against Negroes and poor people.

I've seen it in my own neighborhood, how the colored women take the bus in the early morning to work for white families for low wages. Mrs. Johnson, a big woman, used to come to clean my mother's house once a month. Mrs. Johnson would sit on my bed and say, "How ya doing honey?" She would rub my forehead and say, "Nice girl, I love you, honey." No one else loved me; no one else stroked my head. I loved Mrs. Johnson.

Ernie worked in my father's store on Mulberry Street. Whenever I came by with my mother, Ernie would come out and say, "Hi, my favorite girl, how are you doing today?" Sometimes when my father was busy waiting on customers or out buying goods, Ernie would sit me on his lap and say, "Now, are you being a good girl? You know you're my favorite."

Evie—small frame, big voice—talks about changing the world. "The workers! They're where it's at. The system's fucked!" I want to be around Evie. I don't want to be around my classmates who play bridge and talk about getting married.

Evie and I go to New York together—the Village—she to work, I to a semester at NYU. My father says he will pay for one semester. "Sixteen dollars a credit is a lot," he says. We find a studio apartment for eighty dollars a month on the corner of Christopher and Gay Streets in the heart of Greenwich Village. Evie immediately becomes politically active. Well-known activists, like Tom Hayden and Michael Harrington, hang around our apartment for drink, dope, and talk.

I take a course on changing society. The professor encourages the class to participate. I also join CORE (Congress for Racial Equality) as an extra-curricular activity. We go to a sit-in in Maryland. When we get there, the cops are everywhere, threatening us. I stare at the people in the coffee shop being given directions. Sit still, move, don't move. I feel as if I'm a part of something important happening. When I get back to New York, I report to my class about the sit-in. I was scared, but I wanted the world to change.

Now my professor encourages us to join the cause for voter registration. I sign up to go to Mississippi. No one else in my class signs up. I take a train with some other workers. We're met at the train station, taken to a house, briefed about the dangers, given materials to study. Be careful.

I walk through the town, looking out. Black people. Looking at my skin. Am I black? Where am I? Lost. Lost in the back reaches of my childhood, of Newark, of my father's store. It's all familiar. I keep looking at my skin, not knowing where I am. Where am I? Please tell me.

I try to focus on the voter registration, but I can't. I just walk through the town the first few days, wondering if I'm black. I wander into the voter registration headquarters. James Forman is in charge. He says, "You're going back to New York. Get your stuff. The train leaves at four twenty. I'll take you there."

"No," I say. "I'm here to do voter registration."

"No, you're going on the train."

I walk around that afternoon, waiting, waiting to take the four-twenty train, wondering why I'm not staying. Why? I believe that everyone should vote. They need people to help them sign up. Why can't I stay? I ride that long train ride back to Penn Station in New York.

I go back to my apartment on Christopher and Gay Streets. The apartment is full of Evie's friends. I hear voices talking all day, all night. I hear words—words like racial bigotry, cold war, threat of the bomb. They sit and write, write something they call the Port Huron statement. They're going to start a new movement. They're calling it SDS (Students for a Democratic Society). Tom Hayden, Michael Harrington, and the others are leaving for Michigan.

Activists come to our apartment—SNCC (Student Nonviolent Coordinating Committee) workers, some from the North, some from the South. The SNCC chairman is a black guy named Chuck who's come up from South Carolina. He's good looking, solid, talks to people easily. One night when everyone else goes out to a bar, Chuck and I are alone together. He sits close to me and starts asking me questions. Questions I'm not used to hearing. Where am I from? What do I want to do in the movement? I'm surprised that he's paying attention to me. No one ever seems to care about me. He puts his arm around me. We kiss, and he wants to do more. Is this really happening? We lie down on the couch, but when he gets on top of me, I start screaming. I can't stop. I scream and scream.

He puts his hand over my mouth. "Girl," he says, "you're gonna get me killed. I gotta get out of here."

He leaves. I'm alone. I'm shaking. I don't know where I am. I don't want to live. I take an overdose of sleeping pills. Evie finds me and calls an ambulance. I wind up at St. Vincent's Hospital to get my stomach pumped.

Evie calls my parents, tells them what happened, puts me on a train home. The next day, my parents take me to Dr. Pussin, a well-known psychiatrist for rich women in New Jersey, who says, "Put her away." He tells me he has something new that will help me, something innovative that has helped a lot of his patients. He makes arrangements for me to go to Carrier Clinic in Belle Meade, New Jersey. Quiet bucolic grounds to muffle out the noises in my head. Quiet me, seething with the rage of the early sixties, with the rage at Chuck saying, "Shut up, girl." Rage at men, at my father. My quiet father, barely more than five feet tall, with his dark curly hair, his pants pulled up high, and his "Listen to me. I know what's good for you."

At Carrier Clinic, the doctor's voice is calm, and I'm in pain. I want to try the treatment. I want to try anything that will help me. In the ward at the clinic, I wait for them to come and prep me, but when they lay me on the table and clamp down my hands and clamp my body, even before they begin turning up the voltage, I know it's wrong. I scream, "NO, NO, NO," and start tossing my head, and then I hear a voice say, "She won't go out," and another voice says, "Turn up the voltage," and I'm still not going out. Later I wake up, my hands still tied.

I'm taken back to the ward. I don't know where I am. *I see concrete walls. I see me walking down narrow stairs. I see the basement of my father's store. Someone's coming toward me, throwing me on the ground.* It's so clear, so alive. I want to tell someone. I have an appointment with a therapist. But when I see him, he doesn't want to listen. Instead, he orders Thorazine for me.

It's over. I know it. No one will ever hear me. When I line up for the pills, I take them and hold them in my mouth just long enough to get to a bathroom and throw them down the toilet. I don't know what makes me throw the pills out, but I do. I know I don't want to take Thorazine.

I get out of the mental hospital, go back to Rutgers Newark campus, graduate in 1963, less than a year later. I work for a year as a social worker, living in the East Village, commuting to New Jersey, walking the streets of Springfield Avenue in Newark. Every day, I wear knit suits. Official, businesslike. The streets of Newark smell. The hot streets of the hot tenements on Springfield Avenue where I have a caseload of sixty-plus families within a one-block radius. The tenements reek of live rats crawling over babies in the railroad apartments. Ten children in one room. No stove or refrigerator. I ask my client how she manages. This big buxom woman stares at me, the white social worker. She says, "We get by." She doesn't complain to the white landlord—the downtown white Jewish or Italian landlord that charges six hundred dollars for a rat-infested flat—in 1964.

By the end of the year, I'm carrying my briefcase, walking the streets of the East Village, walking the streets of Newark, singing to myself "We Shall Overcome, We Shall Overcome." I'm trying to hang on.

I'm in trouble. My German psychiatrist tells me I have to be put away again. She wants me to go to Hillsdale Hospital in Queens.

I know I will not survive another mental hospital.

Everyone Needs to Work

&

Portland, 1964. Greg is sitting near Renee playing his guitar. "Union maid who never was afraid … I dreamed I saw Joe Hill last night … as we go marching, marching in the beauty of the day …" I am mesmerized. I love those union songs, I love hearing about working people … working to have better lives and working toward peace and justice and … the worker, the worker is the one. Capitalism is evil.

I know about Greg. Caty talked about him. She would say, "Oh, go see Greg. He'll seduce you." He's about twenty-five, close to my age. He has a boyish look and a boyish body, five feet eight inches. Greg has been living at Renee's for several years now. After his sophomore year of high school, he had been sent to the University of Chicago. He couldn't make the adjustment at such a young age. He wound up trying to slit his wrists and not being able to take care of himself. He also just got out of a TB hospital.

History. People's lives connect. Greg met Renee in Chicago when they were hanging out with theater people on Chicago's Southside. Renee collected people. Greg stayed in her world, and they moved around to Mexico, to New York, back to Chicago, usually with a menagerie of other people. Caty also met Renee in Chicago when she was an aspiring actress in the theatre with people like Ed Asner, Elaine May, and Mike Nichols, before their Second City fame.

Renee creating scenes, tying people together. Renee had adopted Sheila, her sister Tevia's daughter. Now Sheila is pregnant, and the baby needs a name, so Renee has Greg marry Sheila, but they've never had an intimate relationship.

Renee is in the kitchen, playing her autoharp, belting out lyrics to songs she wrote herself, songs about peace and freedom and finding your way. Tom is looking into an empty jar, stoned. Greg is just hanging out by the foot of the bed. A junkie who recently started living here is pacing back and forth. Renee has taken away his drugs. She puts down the autoharp. It's the middle of the night. I want to go to sleep, but I've learned here that I don't go to sleep when I'm tired, only when Renee lets me.

After a month, I settle into the unpredictable routine.

"Okay, it's time you go to work," she says to me. I don't know what she wants me to do this time. Scrub the floor again? I pick up the mop. "Put that down," she screams. "This time you're going to work."

"What do you mean?"

"I mean you need a job, a real job."

"I wouldn't know what to do. I'm a social worker."

"Stupid," she continues, "you aren't going to have some big-shot job. You're going to work—we need some money coming in. You can go down to the temp agency."

"I can barely type," I protest. "I can barely do anything."

"Everyone needs to work. See, I work here all day. It's time you worked. You're going to go to work." She turns to Tom. "Go get that trunk down from the attic—the old one with the trim."

He comes down and puts a big brown leather trunk on the floor.

"Well, we better get you dressed. You can't wear those sloppy pants downtown."

She opens the trunk and starts pulling out outfits, white Mexican blouses that are turning gray, pink polyester tops, A-line skirts.

I don't move.

She takes out a blue polyester blouse and holds it up against me. "Here, put this on." Then she hands me an old-fashioned, plaid wool skirt. "And see if this fits too." I put it over my head, pull down my pants. The blouse is hanging off my shoulder, the skirt, I can't button.

"That's all right," she says, "Keep the blouse on over the skirt and it'll work fine."

I hate these clothes. They remind me of Bergen Street in Newark where my mother took me shopping and made me wear clothes that looked awful. They were good quality, tailored, what everyone wore, but my stomach stuck out. I could never button anything. Why is Renee making me wear these dumb clothes?

"All right, start calling some temp agencies. Get the phone book."

"Renee, it's three o'clock in the morning."

"Don't be stupid. Write down the phone numbers now, and call them when they open in the morning."

In the morning, tired from too little sleep, I start calling. To my surprise, one place tells me they have a job answering phones at an office downtown. I go down to the temp agency, fill out a form, get directions to the job. They tell me to show up the next morning at nine.

That night, Renee keeps me up until three. I wake up for the first day at my new temp job bleary-eyed and tired.

Strange world. Taking the bus to downtown. Leaving Northwest Kearney Street. I've barely left the house except to go to the Laundromat since I arrived three months ago. Lunchtime—I sit in the lunchroom with the others—no other temps. A long table. The girls all dressed in tucked-in blouses with a shiny look and bright colors. Me, in another of Renee's outfits, me sitting at the end of the long table—staring, hearing the girls talk. Boyfriends, husbands, buying a new couch, buying a new blender, talking about last weekend, next weekend. Hearing about moments I don't have. I'm in my own cocoon. No one sits next to me, no one comes up to me, no one introduces herself. I don't look at anyone. I don't belong here. Why don't I ever belong anywhere? I don't have a boyfriend to talk about. I don't ever fit in.

The next morning, Renee pulls a graying Mexican blouse and pair of loose pants from the trunk. "Here, you're wearing these today."

"I can't wear those to the job. Everyone else is wearing nice clothes."

"You're wearing them. It's good for those girls in the office to see something else. It's good for them."

I put them on. Renee won't let me leave. She flits around the kitchen, talking nonstop in her loud, bellowing voice—complaining about how stupid I am, talking about the new junkie staying with us, saying that I should sleep with Greg. When she finally lets me go, I get to my job late. I'm late the next day too, for the same reason.

"Miss Waldman," my supervisor says at the end of the week, "we won't need your services anymore." I knew it. Renee wouldn't let me work, really. She makes a big scene about my going to work, but she doesn't let me work. Renee is worse than my mother. Caty and Nancy are wrong. She's not saving me; she's ruining me. She's ruining my life.

One day I walk into the kitchen, and Renee is on the phone. Her voice boomerangs off the walls. "That's right, Mr. Waldman, she needs a car. We've already got it picked out—a Volkswagen bug, last year's model … Yeah, you need to send the money. Three thousand dollars."

Why is she talking with my father? Where'd she get this idea? I haven't driven for ages. She'd never let me drive anyway.

She slams down the receiver. "Your father is up to his old tricks again, but he's sending the money. We could use a decent-running car around here."

"Renee, what are we going to do with a car? It's just going to get trashed."

"Shut up. It's time for your father to start paying for all the damage he's done. I'm going to milk him. Next week, I'll tell him I want skis."

"You don't ski."

"I told you, you're not going to make sense of your family. Your father doesn't understand paying, so I'm going to get these things. Got that? Now, go get me some tea and don't spill it."

The next day I'm in her bedroom again—the kitchen. She's walking around, her hips swaying, all two hundred twenty-five pounds of her. Today she's wearing clothes—a simple, shapeless dress. She's barefoot.

She stops. "Get me some tea, you hear? Get me tea. That kind over there. No, Greg, you get it. She can't do anything. She can't cook. She can't fuck. You don't know how to get into bed with a man, do you? Look at Greg here, just out of the hospital with TB. Go give him a hug. Do something. You two should get it on. Greg, take her downstairs for God's sake."

He brings Renee the tea, puts down the tray by her bed on the floor. Walks past me, his eyes on the floor, and goes downstairs to his basement room.

"Get out," Renee says to me. "Get out of here." I stand there. Where should I go? Should I go downstairs? Should I go upstairs? What's wrong with me? Why don't I ever sleep with a guy, as Renee says? Everyone sleeps with someone here. Oh, my head spins.

I do go downstairs. Greg ignores me. I can't stand it. Go up to my room. The voices. *You're worthless. Nobody loves you. There's something wrong with you.* I eat bread, bread and butter, upstairs in the little kitchen near my room. Homemade bread. I want it. More than I can say. I eat the whole loaf. It's not enough. It's never enough.

THE BOYFRIEND

§

Hillside, New Jersey, 1955. First year of high school. My friends and I are so excited—Elinor, Harriet, Carol, Deena, Linda. They talk about all the new boys they'll meet. They're all starting to go out on dates. I want to have a boyfriend too. I want to be excited like them.

The school assembly. The freshman class sits in the balcony because we're the largest class. There's no room for us in the main auditorium. Frank, the senior class president, is on stage saying, "The senior class challenges the junior class for the magazine drive."

The speakers continue. "The junior class challenges the sopho-more class." I look around at my classmates. I expect one of the guys to get up and answer the challenge. No one does. I look at Frank, so confident in front of the audience. I say to myself, "If he can do it, I can." So I stand up and shout from the balcony, "The freshman class challenges the senior class." The entire audience gets quiet, and then I hear applause from my freshman class.

After the assembly Frank comes running up to me in the hall. "What made you stand up and challenge us? We didn't challenge the freshman class 'cause we knew you would win. Your class is so much bigger."

I tell him, "You looked so casual—I figured, if you could stand up there, I could stand up."

"Casual?" he says. "Are you kidding? I've been rehearsing for this for two weeks."

The dance. Frank asks me to be his date. I can't believe it. Me, with my hair with split ends. Me, who never got kissed when we played spin the bottle. I have a date with a boy, a popular boy.

I tell my mother I need a new dress for the dance. "I can't take you shopping today," she glares at me. "You know I have to take your brother to the doctor. He was coughing and wheezing all night last night." She pulls out some bills from her purse and shoves them toward me. "Pick out something decent for once."

I go shopping with Deena. I find a white felt skirt and top with gold braiding at the waist and a low-cut neckline. It fits me perfectly because I lost some weight during the summer. I'm so proud. I feel like I fit in.

At home, I try on the dress in my room. My mother stomps in and looks at me. "You look like a whore!" she screams. She calls in the neighbor, Mrs. Reiman, who is a dressmaker. Together they sit on my twin bed and alter the neckline on the dress. It looks awful.

Frank doesn't mind. He's so easy going. We spend a lot of time together after that. Whenever my friends are hanging out with their boyfriends, he's with me. We sometimes double date with Deena and her boyfriend Mike. We hold hands in the back seat of Mike's car. One night he leans over and kisses me on the mouth—not a soul kiss—our mouths are closed. But for me, it means I finally have a real boyfriend.

One evening soon after that, I'm waiting by the front door for Frank to pick me up. My mother calls down to me from her bedroom, "Come here."

"I can't," I say. "I'm going out."

"Come up here right now!"

"I'll come later when I get home."

"Do you hear me, young lady? Get up here now. You're not going out with Frank."

I climb the steps to the second floor of our house. I look into my mother's room. She's lying on top of the bed, naked. Stark naked. Her eyes have a distant look—a weird look. I freeze at the doorway. What is going on with her?

She gets up from the bed and stands by the dresser. "I have something to say to you. You have to start thinking about your future. We're Jewish. Frank is Catholic. It's time you thought of these things."

"I'll think about it, but I gotta go now."

"You're not going out with Frank"

"But I have a date tonight."

"You don't. I called him and told him you can't see him anymore. It's for your own good."

"You what?"

I rush out of the room, call Frank, and say, "Don't believe my mother."

He says we're not going out and hangs up the phone. What did she say to him?

My insides want to die. I can't believe my mother. She's crazy. I want Frank. I want to have a boyfriend. He liked me. I liked him. I'm stuck. Stuck with my mother. I know I'll never have a boyfriend again, never.

WHO WOULD MARRY HER?

༄

Hillside, New Jersey, 1957. Sixteen years old. Junior year in high school. My mother is driving me crazy. Shopping with her is a nightmare. Ohrbach's, Klein's, Hahne's. It doesn't matter. With her jaw set tight, she stands me in front of the sales girl, pulls at the skirt I'm trying on, and screams, "Nothing fits you! You're too fat!" She walks away and leaves me standing there.

I can't do anything right. I have to get out of the house. I join B'nai Brith Girls. I become the regional vice president. On weekends, I travel to Pennsylvania and southern New Jersey. I run for office in the clubs at school. I stay after school every day.

My mother screams, "You're doing too much!"

My body rebels. Swollen stomach. Eyes bulging. Lump in my throat. Taken to the doctor. Toxic goiter. Graves disease. I gain forty pounds in two months. My thyroid has to come out.

"Who's going to marry her?" my mother screams.

Beth Israel Hospital. I see doctors. Lots of them. I see Dr. Seidman, who brought me into this world. My mother keeps badgering him, "The scar's gonna show; it's gonna show!"

After the surgery, Dr. Seidman measures my neck, puts pearls around it.

"See," he reassures my mother. "The scar won't show."

I come back to school after my surgery. My friends are dating, talking about clothes and makeup. Elinor, Carol, Harriet. Their conversation is all about their boyfriends. They live in the world of rock 'n' roll, dresses, parties. Their mothers buy them the right clothes, encourage them in their social lives. But I walk through the halls of Hillside High with my belly sticking out, wearing the same plaid skirt every day. I don't talk about boys. I'm different. The usual high school things—songs, games, meeting in Mike's Coffee Shop—I'm not part of that.

My mother screams on the phone to relatives. She says, "Look what I have to put up with! A sick son, a crazy daughter."

I know my mother never wanted to get married. She's always saying, "I liked working. I liked going out on weekends with my friends. My cousins pushed me into marrying your father." My father acts as if he doesn't hear her. Neither one of them is there for me.

I want to tell everyone what it's like walking through the halls, stomach sticking out, and eyes bulging. All alone. Dark halls. Dark clothes. Swollen neck. Swollen belly. I cry out inside.

After the operation, I get sicker and sicker. My mother takes me to Lahey Clinic in Boston. The doctors examine me and say the operation was a success. They don't give me any medication to replace the hormones produced by the thyroid. I read the report. All it says is that I have severe emotional problems.

By senior year, I'm even more alone. Mrs. Polsinelli takes me in hand. She makes me co-editor-in-chief of the yearbook and keeps me by her side so I can graduate.

THE FIRST TIME

⅋

Israel, 1959. Eighteen years old. After high school graduation, I spend the summer in Israel. It's the first time I've ever been out of New Jersey. Now the summer is nearly over. Soon I'll be going back to New Jersey to start my freshman year at Douglass College, Rutgers University's all girls' school.

Tonight, I'm sitting in an open field with my group, with our leaders. We're singing, playing drums, guitars—singing songs about Israel, the pioneers, building the land. I look around me. Bodies are swaying. My heart wants to open. I feel connected, warm for maybe the first time in my life.

After the singing, I start talking with this guy named Jack. I find out he's a Hashomer Hatzair, a political leftist. He tells me about the workers—the workers have rights, the workers matter. I feel the same way. He's wearing sabra clothes and sandals. He moves his body like a sabra.

We walk. We talk. He holds my hand. He's much older than I am, about twenty-eight. I'm wearing my sabra shorts. My stomach sticks out. Why does he want to be with me? I'm fat. I'm ugly. But I want so much for someone to want me, to love me. He tries to get me to come back to his apartment. "Please," he says. What does he want?

He takes me to his room. A room upstairs on a narrow street in a Yemenite neighborhood. He kisses me. I don't feel passion. I don't feel anything. He takes off my clothes. I can't breathe. He says we can go slow. "Stop!" I scream. My mind goes blank. I just start screaming and screaming, "Let me out. Let me out." *Loud screams come from deep inside of me. I've got to get out of here.*

Suddenly I hear men chanting outside, men banging pots. Up and down the narrow street. Men's voices. Ah, ah, ah. Banging on pots. Jack tells me it's a Yemenite tradition when a girl loses her virginity. I want to crawl under the bed and stay there. I want to die. My face is frozen—frozen in the shame. What's wrong with me?

Jack gets dressed. I get dressed. He walks me back to the house where I'm staying. "Please stay here in Israel with me," he says. What should I do? He says he wants me. But I'm supposed to go to college. I feel torn apart. I can't stay.

A week later, I'm standing in a room full of freshman girls from all over New Jersey and Long Island. They're in sweaters and skirts. I'm in sabra shorts. We have tea. The dean and the teachers are there. I see white gloves. We're supposed to wear white gloves at the tea. I stand by myself.

My head is spinning. Where am I? I'm in Israel. Where is Jack? Why am I here? I belong in Israel. I've got to see Jack. I've got to get out of here. I write to him. I try calling. He doesn't answer. I'm alone in a sea of voices, sounds that nothing will drown out.

My body is stiff. I move aimlessly from place to place. I go to classes. Please, God, help me. I can't focus. I can't study. I've got to find Jack. My dorm mates all have boyfriends. They come in just before the eleven o'clock curfew. They can't wait to get out for the weekend.

I'm by myself. I sit in the library. I'm alone, and the nighttime is the worst. The sweat of the night. The sweat of the aloneness, staring at the ceiling. *I see circles around and around the long corridor of my dorm. I see men coming at me. I see big bodies moving in. I want to run. I've got to get out of here. The dark walls, the narrow halls. The dark walls move, move toward me. The narrow halls are closing in. Someone's coming after me. He's going to get me. "Please, mister, don't. Please."*

I scream. "Let me out. Let me out." I run up and down the hall. I rip off my clothes. I run naked through the dorm. I can't stand it here. I've got to move to another dorm. The dean calls my parents. I'm moved to a small house dorm that doesn't have a long dark hallway. It's better. I don't scream. I sit on my bed, try to study, and wear the same jeans and top every day for months. I don't wash. I don't go outside except to classes. I just stare. Israel is far away in my mind. I am far away. Away.

UP THE MOUNTAIN

☙

Portland, 1964. I wake up to Renee shouting, "We're going out today. It's after Thanksgiving." You can hear her voice all through the house.

"Tom and I are taking a little trip to Mt. Hood. You and Greg are coming. I can't leave you alone."

We drive off in the yellow VW Renee bought with the money my father sent. Our only trip out of Portland, out of Northwest Kearney Street. We go up the mountain for the day. We walk around the visitor area. We see the tall trees, see paths to walk, feel the earth underneath—the raw earth, walking, feeling my feet move, feeling alive.

When we get home, Renee says, "Greg, take her downstairs. Tom and I need to be alone for a while."

"Come on," Greg says.

We don't talk much. Mostly he plays his guitar and sings in a soft voice. He plays union songs, political songs, Pete Seeger songs. I'm happy just to sit and listen and watch him play songs I love to hear, songs about freedom, songs about another way to be in this world.

When it gets late, Greg puts the guitar down and gets into his bed, a single mattress on the floor, pushed up against the wall. "You can stay here if you want," he says.

"Okay." I crawl in beside him.

We lie there. I take off my top. Greg is beside me, but he doesn't move. I'm drifting off to sleep.

"That was a nice day up the mountain," Greg whispers. "We should do that more often." He rolls over close, slides my underwear off, climbs on top of me. I feel him take his penis out of his pajamas. He's aroused. Then he's in me. I don't feel anything. He moves around, gets excited, comes. Finally he sighs and rolls off. We don't talk, don't kiss, don't hold each other. I fall asleep.

Later in the night, Greg wakes me up. "It's getting late," he says. "We should get some sleep. Maybe you better go upstairs."

I crawl off his single mattress on the basement floor and walk up the stairs by myself. I get into bed alone.

About two months later, in January when it's cold and dreary outside, my stomach hurts. A shooting pain, a hardness. Renee yells at me from the kitchen to bring her something, a dish, a book, a pan, something. I'm doubled over. The shooting pain in my stomach. I have a tumor. I'm going to die. No one cares about me.

"What's the matter with you?" Renee says, angry.

"Stomach hurts," bending over and clutching my belly.

"We've got to get you to the doctor. Look at you. You're eating too much bread. You're sluggish. Look at all that fat on you. I'm going to call the doctor so you can get a checkup."

I go back to my room, and she yells to me later, "Okay. I got you an appointment for tomorrow at ten o'clock in the morning. The lady doctor I told you about down the street. She's retired. She doesn't see patients anymore, but she'll see you. Understand? Tom will walk over there with you. You can see the doctor by yourself, and then I want you to come right back."

I wait in the waiting room. A Victorian house with dark wood paneling, with dark burgundy walls, with high ceilings. I wait. She calls my name. She's a tall elderly woman with short, curly white hair. She's not wearing a white jacket. She's wearing a sweater and black skirt.

She tells me to get up on the table. I tell her my stomach hurts. She tells me to pull up the white sheet and puts my feet into the stirrups. She feels around with a speculum. "Get dressed." She takes me into another dark room. "You're pregnant. Renee told me you're not married. Why don't you come back tomorrow with Renee, and I'll give you a D & C. Be here at eleven."

I walk out in a daze. Pregnant? How can I be pregnant? I run back to Renee's. She's at the front door waiting.

"Pregnant?" she says. "Who have you been running around with? Pregnant? We can't have another pregnant woman in this house. Sheila is already pregnant, and one is enough. You better get yourself out of this. You're going back to see that doctor tomorrow."

I lie down on my bed. I can't be pregnant. It's a mistake. There can't be a baby growing inside me.

The next morning, Renee walks me back to the retired doctor's house. She says Tom will pick me up in a couple of hours. She talks to the doctor. The doctor explains the procedure—just a scraping of the uterus.

A strong feeling rises up inside me and says no. I say, "I can't do this." I open the old oak door and run out. I run back to Renee's, climb the stairs, and get into bed.

I hear her heavy footsteps coming up the stairs for me.

"You're getting a D & C," she says.

"I don't want one."

"You need one."

I don't answer. I stare out the window.

My belly hurts, my belly is getting hard, but I don't really believe I'm pregnant. Renee keeps screaming. "Greg isn't the father. You're lying!"

I shake my head. "It has to be Greg."

"Are you the father?" she asks Greg.

He shrugs. "I have TB."

"She's lying. You're not the father. She doesn't know what she's talking about."

"Whatever you say, Renee," Greg shrugs again.

Renee turns back to me. "You're a liar," she shouts. "It was that guy you brought home that night—the longshoreman. He's the father. What's his name? I'll find him."

Renee insists the father is this longshoreman who gave me a ride home one night. Renee insists Greg is married to Sheila. Sheila's pregnant, but Greg isn't the father. Renee screams at me and says I can't stay here and have the baby. A baby? I can't think about a baby. I can't think about being pregnant. I look down and see blood seeping through my pants. Renee sees it too. "Tom," she shouts, "get her to the hospital."

It's late, very late at night. Tom drives me in his pickup. We wait hours. Time crawls. A young doctor examines me. Strapped to the stirrups. Lights overhead.

"Miss Waldman?" Doctors surround me. The doctor says, "You're almost three months pregnant. Why did you try to abort your baby?" Abort? What is he talking about? I didn't do anything. Tom takes me home. For a week, I stay in bed. I don't get up except to go to the bathroom and eat. The bleeding stops.

THE DARK PLACE

❧

Newark, New Jersey, October 1944. Three and a half years old.
Old wooden door with kick marks.

Ninety-three Mulberry Street, Waldman Brothers, butter, cheese, and eggs.

Don't open, do open.

Her daddy tells her not to go down there, to the basement, to the dark basement, the smelly basement.

She's at her daddy's store today because her mommy is in the hospital having a new brother or sister for her. Her daddy is so busy. He tells her, "Stay out of the way."

No one wants her here. She wants to play.

Now the door is open a little bit. She wonders what is there. She looks down. It's dark. She hears voices. Shouting. "Over here to the left. Stack it up high. Hurry up, we don't have all day. What's the matter with you guys? You think this is a play field?"

She takes a few steps into the dark. She holds onto the rail. She hears strange noises. Boxes being moved around. The chute. It makes the boxes go down fast. She can hear the click, click, clack of the metal rollers.

She keeps taking the steps, one by one very slowly. The steps are wide and far apart. There is empty space between the steps. Why is everything so big?

Now she sees light. It comes from the open cellar door.

So she walks down the steps. One by one. She wants to see the men working. She wants to find Ernie. Ernie is a really nice man. His skin is very dark, and his teeth are white. Ernie likes her. He always puts her on his knee and says, "How is my favorite little girl doing today?" But Ernie isn't here today.

She walks down to the bottom of the steps and hides behind a sack of beans. There are big sacks, little sacks, red beans, yellow beans, brown beans. No one sees her. They are so busy shouting.

All of a sudden the noises stop. The boxes stop coming down the chute, and the men stop shouting. It seems as if everyone has disappeared.

"Hey, little girl, what are you doing in here? Hey, man, look what we have here. The boss's daughter."

The door to the chute is closed. There is no light. What is happening? She stands behind a box. It's fun behind the box. All her playmates can come out and play now. *Here, Junipee and Marge and Zastopel.* They understand her. They come out and play.

"Up against the wall. Put her up against the wall."

The wall feels cold and wet. It's the concrete stone. Against the wall, her skirt flies up. "Come here, little girl."

She is just here to play, she knows that.

Here, Junipee and Marge and Zastopel. Let's go outside and play. We'll show them now. You be good children and come out with me. We're going to take a walk out in the fresh sunlight. My playmates want to play with me. I am not here. Can't you see, mister? My playmates want to go outside and play with me. Tra la la fa la la, light and gay I will play. I have so many friends. I am a good little girl. And my friends want to come out and play with me. We're going out into the sunshine right now. Can't you see this is no place for a child? A growing child. My friends say we must go outside immediately. Let us go outside. It is too dark in here. They are my friends. Let them go outside. You don't want to keep them here, do you, mister? No, you wouldn't want to do that.

What are you doing, mister? Why are you acting like that? My daddy wouldn't like that one bit. Who are you? Are you my daddy? My daddy is going to come. The wall. The ceiling. The floor. Twirling around patterns. Why doesn't someone come and get me?

Suddenly her daddy is standing over her. He shakes her. He screams, "Get up! Look at you. Get upstairs!"

He's mad, my daddy. He's going to kill me.

"Get upstairs if you know what's good for you, young lady. Get upstairs."

THE TRUTH

&

Newark, New Jersey, 1956. Fifteen years old. Sophomore year at Hillside High. I'm required to take a science, biology. Mr. Duthie announces to the class we have to do a biology project to get our grade. We can dissect a frog; we can build a skeleton—anything as long as it is related to biology, the body. "Be creative," he says.

My classmates get busy. I know I don't want to look at bones or a skeleton. The tangible elements of a science project don't excite me. I sit at my desk wondering, and in that moment, a thought comes to me. Biology. Life. My body. That's biology, I think. I will tell a story. I will write my life story. I'm so excited about doing something no one else would think of.

I get busy. It's easy. The words pour out of me. I tell the story of my family, the Waldman family. Me, a child of an immigrant. I'm proud of my father, buying a grocery store for two hundred dollars when he was fifteen years old. He works so hard; he never has time for me. But he cares about me. I know he does. I remember the summer he tried so hard to win the doll for me on the Boardwalk. He stood for hours tossing the ball into the ring until he finally won.

But sometimes I don't know who he is. When I was little, he held me, he held me so tight, he touched me, he kissed me all over. My

Uncle Sydney died in the war, a telegram was delivered to the house, my father cried, "Hold me, hold me." I didn't like him touching me.

He never touches me now. But I think he comes into my room in the early morning and looks at me. My body stiffens. What does he want? What am I supposed to do? I stare out the window by my bed. All I see are the leaves on the elm tree outside. I don't dare look at him.

I write about my brother Paul, three and a half years younger than me. Wrapped in gauze his first year because of eczema. Then it turned into asthma. Trips to Beth Israel Hospital in the middle of the night. Is he going to die? Me, watching over him at home. He can't breathe. I don't want him to die.

Maybe I shouldn't write about these things. I know! I'll change the names so it will be a work of fiction! No one will know. My brother Paul I call Peter, and I am Jean, and I write upstairs in my room at 1500 Munn Avenue, sitting at my built-in desk that covers the radiator. I write every day. I come home from school and write. I want to tell. I want to be heard.

I type up a twenty-five-page document with carbon copies, and I'm so proud. I bring it in to school. Mr. Duthie says, "What's this?"

"It's my life story," I say.

He takes it with the skeletons, with the dissected frogs.

A few days later, Mr. Duthie says, "Please go down to the principal's office."

I'm a good student. Why am I being called to the principal's office?

I walk in. My parents are sitting there at two thirty Tuesday afternoon. What is going on? My father never leaves work early. The school psychologist, a fat perspiring man is also there, and Mr. Custer, the principal. Mr. Duthie walks in too.

"Sit down, Miss Waldman," the psychologist says to me. "Miss Waldman, we have your biology project here. Why did you write this?"

I say that the mind is also biology, and I wanted to tell my story. The school psychologist looks weird. He is sweating. He doesn't look at me. He is looking at my parents.

"Miss Waldman, your father is a good, hardworking man. Why did you tell these lies? Miss Waldman, this paper is full of lies. It's not a biology project; it's lies. I know you are a good student, so we won't flunk you, but you are never to write again. Do you hear me, young lady? You are never to write these lies again. Never. I've discussed this with Mr. Duthie, and he will give you a C-, and you are not to discuss this with anyone. Now, your parents care about you and cared enough to come today, and we want you to apologize to them when you go home. You can leave now with your parents."

Mr. Custer has my paper. I don't ask for it back. I go home and want to find my story. I search the house for the carbons. I look in my desk, I look in the attic, but the carbon copies aren't anyplace. I dream about the carbons. I get up in the night looking for the carbons. I think that, maybe, I forgot a spot where they might be.

I try to remember, "What did I write in that paper?" The story of my family. My father coming to America. My mother born in New York, raised by a single working mother in a household that didn't speak English. My brother Paul, who has had asthma since he was a year old. My father coming into my room in the early morning at 1500 Munn Avenue. My father's store at 93 Mulberry Street in Newark, where I played as a young girl and where I went down into the basement, the dark place, and my father came down screaming, "Put your panties on!"

I search everywhere, looking all over for those carbon copies, and they're gone, and I know that a part of me is missing, that the truth of my life at 1500 Munn Avenue with my name changed to Jean is nowhere to be found, and I can't remember anything, and that big fat psychologist that sweated and didn't know anything told me I was never to write again.

GETTING SANE

※

Portland, 1964. Renee screams at me, "Get out of here. You're too much of a nuisance up here."

I go downstairs. Greg and I don't talk.

"Bring me some wood," Renee shouts down the stairs.

Greg picks at the woodpile, gathers an armload of split logs for the wood stove. He sees me and throws a piece of wood at my stomach. It misses me, falling to the floor.

I've had enough. Out. I want out. Outside. I run. It's freezing, but I don't care. I run down Northwest Kearney Street in my nightgown. Greg runs after me, catches up, grabs me by the arm.

"What are you doing? You can't just run off like this."

My hair is blowing, my eyes are huge. "Leave me alone."

"Come back."

"No, I'm leaving."

"You can't run away with just your nightgown on."

"I don't care. I'm leaving."

Tom comes with the truck. They sandwich me in the middle between them. Back to Renee's.

"You can't stay here," Renee shouts. "You can't stay here and have a baby." She yells some more, "What are you going to do?" I can't stay there, but she won't let me leave. I don't know what I'm going to do. I don't know.

Renee takes me to downtown Portland to see a psychiatrist she knows. She shows up in her muumuu. She talks. She walks back and forth and talks to the psychiatrist, talks around him, through him. Words. Big words, little words. She tells him that I can't stay with her anymore—Sheila is pregnant, and that's enough. Greg is married to Sheila, and that's enough.

Renee points to me and says to the psychiatrist, "I can't do anything with her. The others who come through—after a while they get well enough and run away. This one can't. She's too crazy. She's not capable of being on her own. And now she wants to have a baby. Besides, she's still legally in her parents' custody. She was in a mental hospital back East a few years ago and, from what I can figure out, was released to her parents at that time."

Renee talks circles around the psychiatrist, a small man in a dark suit with a dark tie. She convinces him I need to go to Dammash, the Oregon State Mental Hospital.

"Just for a short stay," she says to me. "You'll have to admit yourself. When you check out, your name will be cleared. Your parents won't have custody anymore."

I have nowhere to go. Renee figures out I should go to Dammash.

⅋

I don't think they'll take me. I'm not crazy. Waiting, the eternity of waiting for the admissions. I'm given a clipboard with a form. I take the stubby pencil and mark yes/no over and over. They take me.

"OK," the nurse says when I'm done. "You can come with me."

I follow her through a door, up a flight of stairs, into a small room with two beds. On one bed is a white hospital gown.

"This will be your room. Please undress and put this on." She leaves.

I'm stunned. I can't believe they took me. I can't believe I'm here.

I room with a girl my age, Susan, with frizzy brown hair. We become friends. She just had a baby. Her husband's parents have the baby now. The nurses give us jobs. We're to clean the toilets. We're to work together. We swish the cleaner around the bowls and flush, talking all the time. We plot that when we get out we'll be together. She tells me she probably won't keep the baby. There are plans for her mother-in-law to keep the baby. I don't have a mother-in-law to keep my baby.

I'm just beginning to show. I feel the baby kick. Some of the other girls are pregnant too. I see them flirting with the guys in the day room, tossing their heads, brushing their bangs out of their eyes. One of the girls has a boyfriend here. I know. I can tell. I want a boyfriend too.

I do make friends with a tall, quiet guy with long fingernails. He plays the guitar. He's not really a boyfriend, but he likes me to sit by him and listen as he plays. I like to listen to him. He asks me to stay around so he can play some more for me. I do. I'm listening to him play when the big red-headed nurse approaches.

"Miss Waldman, you haven't been taking your medicine." She's holding something behind her back.

I stand up and back away.

I see it. She's got a big fat needle in her hand. I see it coming toward me.

I run down the hall. Run away from the cabinet with the sterile needles in the drawer, run away from the red-headed nurse who is following me down the hall.

"Miss Waldman, you have to take your shot."

"No, no, no. The baby. No shots when you're pregnant. That's what I've read. I won't have a shot." The big nurse reaches for me. I duck. An orderly comes after me, corners me, holds me down. She jams the needle in my arm.

"The baby will die. You're killing my baby."

"Now, Miss Waldman," I hear, "we'll take you to your room. Everything will be all right. We have to do what's best for you here, understand?"

I spit at her. The spit goes right into her face. She wipes it away with a tissue.

"Take her back to her room," she tells the orderly.

Later, I wake up in my bed, wet. I peed in the bed. I want to get out of here. Don't they see? They're going to kill my baby. My baby will die. Die, die, die.

I'm lying in my bed, staring at the ceiling.

"Miss Waldman, I need you to come with me." The big red-headed nurse stands in the doorway. She walks beside me, holding my arm tight. We go to the office of the psychiatrist, an older, balding man. He beckons me to sit in the chair in front of his desk. The nurse sits in the corner.

The psychiatrist dials his phone, says hello. "Yes, Mr. Waldman, she's here now.

He extends the phone to me.

My father's voice. "Joan, you're coming home to New Jersey. Arrangements are being made with Greystone Hospital."

"No!" I shout. "You're going to kill my baby!"

"Nonsense. The baby will be fine. You'll put it up for adoption, find a good home."

I know he really wants to kill the baby.

"There're a few matters to attend to, a legal procedure. Then you'll be coming home. Do you hear me?"

I don't answer. *Daddy knows too much. Daddy doesn't want me to tell. He wants me put away.*

The psychiatrist talks with my father. "I totally understand, Mr. Waldman. Yes, could be very expensive to keep her institutionalized. In my opinion she's one of the most disturbed patients ever to come to Dammash." More talking back and forth. "Frankly, I see no hope. That's right. I expect we will be looking at a permanent commitment."

The psychiatrist finishes up with my father and looks at me.

"No," I say before he has a chance to speak. "You can't kill my baby."

"No one intends to kill your baby, Miss Waldman," he says in his all-knowing voice. "We only want to help you. Now, you will be going back to New Jersey to receive treatment and be near your parents. First there's a minor legal procedure to take care of. It's nothing important. Do you understand?"

Oh yes, I understand. They're going to take my baby away.

༄

I'm sitting at a table in a corner of the dining room. Mealtimes are trying for me. I hold the fork, but the food won't reach my mouth—food, fork, mouth. I can't make the connection.

Two policewomen enter the large room. The room, filled with babbling patients and staff, becomes quiet, real quiet. The policewomen start walking in my direction. I don't move. I know. I know they are coming for me. One policewoman reaches for my hands. I don't resist. I am handcuffed.

They lead me across the silent room. The red-headed nurse is waiting at the door, watching me. Everyone is watching me. Something snaps in me. I know that I have to get sane. This is my last mental hospital, my last chance. If I don't figure out what these people want, my life will be over.

"Miss Waldman, we need to take you to the courthouse for a hearing." She gets the black keys at the black desk, and they walk me to a black state vehicle. The nurse drives. One policewoman sits next to her, and I'm in the back with the other.

A voice in my head keeps repeating, "This is your last chance. Hang on. You'll be all right." We drive and drive. We don't stop, not even once, although I have to go to the bathroom. I don't dare ask.

We enter the courthouse through a side door. There's a judge in a black robe, no jury. "Please sit down, Miss Waldman," I hear the judge say. Where is the bench? How do I sit down? Oh, this is awful. I want to pee.

"Sit down," I hear again. The policewoman points to the bench behind me, and I connect with sitting on the bench.

The judge speaks. "This is a court of law. You've been called here for a sanity hearing. This hearing will determine whether you are to be legally committed to the state mental hospital system, in which case you will be sent to the Greystone Park Psychiatric Hospital in Hanover Township, New Jersey. You're to answer the questions I ask, to the best of your ability. You are to tell the truth. Do you understand?

The truth? Whose truth? My truth? My daddy's truth? I know I must answer from another part of me. I must answer what they want to hear, not the truth truth.

If I don't figure out what they want, my life will be shattered, broken apart, melted down, melted through the opening, through the shining diamond rings waving through, waiving my rights, waving me to the back wards of life, waving me from the very basics of life …

"Here's the first question. We see that you were involved in the civil rights movement. Tell us what you did and what your involvement is now."

I want to tell him about the sit-ins, about how the police threatened us in Maryland, about the Freedom Rides in Mississippi. I want to tell him the world is fucked; the Civil Rights Movement is where it's at.

"That's all behind me, Your Honor," I say. "I intend to lead a quiet life now. I will not participate again." The words come out of my mouth, but I don't know where they come from.

"Next question. What do you intend to do with your baby?"

"Oh, the baby's father and I are planning to get married."

"How will you support yourself?"

"I have a part-time job waiting for me when I get out. It doesn't pay well, but I'll find a better one later. I have a college education, and so does the baby's father. He's looking for work now." Am I really saying this? I know the state doesn't want to pay.

The judge asks me to wait in the hallway for a few minutes. I tell the policewoman I have to pee. She takes me to the bathroom. Because I'm in handcuffs, she lifts my dress. *Why are you doing that, mister? I don't think my daddy would let you do that.* I pee. I don't cry. She leads me back to the courtroom.

I stand in front of the judge alone, all alone.

"You've made mistakes in the past, Miss Waldman, but your future seems pointed in the right direction. You answered the questions quite well. I am declaring you sane, capable of returning to normal society. You're free to go." Wham—bangs his gavel. "Good luck to you." He tells the red-headed nurse to take me back to the hospital so I can gather my belongings.

The red-headed nurse spins around and brushes past, refusing to look at me. "Get in the car," she snaps. The policewoman unlocks my handcuffs.

I'm free, the judge said. Free from what? Free from my father? Free to go where? What is sane? What's going to happen to me now? What's going to happen to the baby? *Daddy will be mad. He wants me put away.*

When we get to Dammash, the red-headed nurse says, "You can get your things." I walk in, and Renee and Tom are there. Renee is walking up and down the hall in her muumuu, her body shifting with each step. She comes right up to me.

"Get your things, but you can't stay at the house anymore. I told you. You're free to go now. You're not a ward of the court, and you're not in your parents' custody. Got that? You can stay the night, but you've got to leave tomorrow."

We get back to the house, Greg walks by me, doesn't say a word. Renee goes right to the kitchen and starts moving pots around, getting ready to cook, walking back and forth.

"You're going back to New York. Go to Caty's."

"I don't have any money."

"I've got that worked out. You're taking a Greyhound bus. Tom and I will give you a ride there in the morning and help you buy a ticket. Pack what you'll need. It's a four-day ride." Renee has everything planned, including when the bus leaves.

The next morning, before I leave, she reaches up and takes an autoharp down from a hook on the wall and puts it into my hands. I look at her, surprised. Tom carries the autoharp and drives me to the station. He hands me the autoharp as I get on the bus. I take the first seat and put my bag on the floor. The autoharp sits on my bulging stomach. Tight. Hold the autoharp. Hold the baby. Empty seats, empty spaces, empty world. I want to stop. Hours of dark night. Starting and stopping. Passengers come and go.

My stomach starts to hurt. The pain gets worse. Is the baby coming? I'm going to have the baby on the bus. Should I tell the driver? Should I tell him to let me out, let me out, let me out? The pain goes away.

"Change buses," the driver says somewhere in Nevada. I wait. I don't want to be here. I want to go home. I don't have a home. Big belly, no home, no place to go. New bus. New seat. My little bag, my big stomach, the autoharp—my baby. My insides go up and down with the bus. *I've got to get out of here. Let me out. Daddy, help me get out.*

I look out the bus window. Open space. Dusty brown world. More open space. I don't know where I am. More passengers. A man with a gun in a holster, cowboy boots and spurs, fringed leather jacket. I'm in a John Wayne movie. I clutch the autoharp tight.

I hear the bus driver. "Laramie, Wyoming. Miss, you need to change buses here." I grab my bag and autoharp and get off the bus.

I sit outside on a bench and cry. I can't do this. I can't. At the coffee shop, I get a handful of quarters and dial Renee's.

"Please," I say, "I can't go on. There are cowboys here. I can't make it."

A sigh. Renee's voice isn't as gruff as usual. "All right. Go to the ticket counter. Tell them you want to trade in your ticket to New York for a ticket back to Portland."

Once again, Tom picks me up. We don't talk at all on the way back to the house.

Renee is loud and angry. "You can't stay here" is the first thing she says when she sees me. "Tom, just leave her stuff there by the door. She's not staying."

We go into the kitchen.

"If you can't take the bus, you'll have to fly."

"I don't have money for that."

"Oh, I'll get it all right." She dials the phone, waits. "Mrs. Waldman? It's Renee. Yes. It's important." She waits, and I know the phone is being handed over to my father.

"I'm sending her back to you. She can't take the bus, so you'll have to send money for a plane ticket. You'll need to wire it. We need it right away."

After six months of Renee's insisting that he pay for a car, a typewriter, skis, and whatever else, my father doesn't question her.

Renee hangs up. "That settles it. You're flying back. But listen, this is important. I'm getting you a flight to Idlewild, not Newark."

"My parents are closer to Newark."

"That's the point. You're not going to your parents. You're going to Caty's. Got that?

"What do you mean? My father is sending money for me to go home."

"No, he's sending money for you for go to New York. Listen, stupid—if you go back to them, you won't make it out. They'll lock you up in Greystone. Do not go back to them! Got that? Just call Caty or Tevia, and they'll help you. Understand? Do not go back to your parents!"

PART 2

&

REACHING OUT

CATY TAKES OVER

☙

New York, April 1965. I wander down Fourteenth Street. I'm free. Finally. Free from Renee, from hospitals, from my parents. I'm here by myself. A moment of just being, being alive. Horns honking, buses passing, people perched on the curb waiting to cross. I'm wearing my smocked green dress and a black sweater. That's all I have. Union Square. I'm glad to be home.

Caty finds me in front of Gimbels. She's wearing a thrift store house dress and Zorrie flip-flops. Caty's her own person. She doesn't dress like my friends in New Jersey.

"Where have you been?" she demands, her hands waving around in the air. "Renee said you'd be here hours ago."

I shrug. "It's not so easy to get here from Idlewild."

She takes me to the East Village where she lives with Steve and their little boy, John, who's now two and a half years old. We walk through the cluttered streets, past the shops with junk for sale stacked up on the sidewalk.

Caty is talking nonstop. Caty, the actress who's not an actress. She says her wealthy Midwestern parents wouldn't let her be an actress. But she's always on stage. Tall, willowy, with stringy blond hair. Everything is a big deal with her, a major production.

We stop at Steve's coffee shop on East Tenth Street to pick up John and then walk down the street to Caty and Steve's apartment, littered with diapers and toys. That night I hear Caty and Steve fight. Shouts from behind closed doors. Early the next morning, Caty shouts, "Get up! We gotta get out of here. I can't put up with his bullshit."

We crash with Renee's sister, Tevia. The apartment is small, and John runs all over the place. Tevia doesn't want us there. After two days, she flips out and yells at us, "Get out now!" Caty gathers her few belongings, and the three of us leave—Caty, John, and me.

We walk down East Tenth Street. We walk with no place to go. We walk in the rain, Caty, carrying John on her hip. In front of us, Caty sees a guy she knows. He's blond with piercing blue eyes.

"Dau!" she shouts. Her face lights up.

We stop. They talk. Dau motions for us to follow him. The rain is coming down in hard drops now. We turn down Avenue D. I've never been this far down on the Lower East Side before. I'm chilled and tired, and I have to go to the bathroom. I try to hold it in, but it trickles down my leg.

Dau stops in front of a red brick building. It looks abandoned. It's a squatter's building. Dau says the city owns it and no one lives here. We go inside. We step into a dark hallway. It smells moldy. No lights. We go up a flight and another flight and another. There's gum stuck to the banister, cigarette butts on the steps, and "Join the Revolution!" pamphlets strewn around the hallways.

We stop in front of a door. It's unlocked. "You can stay here," Dau says. "Go in and wait for me. I'll be back." There's nothing in the apartment except trash—no furniture, no food, no place to sleep. I flip a light switch on the wall. Nothing. In the kitchen, Caty turns a handle and water sputters out of a faucet. "Yea! We have water!" she shouts.

John is screaming. Caty takes a baby bottle from the paper bag she's carrying, removes the cap and screws on a nipple. She sits on the floor, puts the nipple in John's mouth. He sucks. All of a sudden it gets quiet, real quiet.

"Caty, this is crazy," I say. "There's no furniture, no nothing."

"We can stay here for awhile," Caty says. "I don't know how, but we'll manage. You gotta get dry. We gotta get you some dry clothes."

"It stinks in here," I tell Caty.

"We can clean it up," she says. "We'll just get rid of all this stuff. Here, hold John for a while."

Caty. I've got to follow her. She always seems to know what to do. She sent me to Renee when the therapist threatened to put me away. I don't know what else I could have done. At least I don't have to go back to my parents. I trust her. I've got to trust her. I remember when I first met her in the East Village coffee shop. I'd come in from my job as a social worker, wearing my knit suits and high heels. She talked to me about art, theatre, the world. She had answers to questions I hadn't even thought of. She cares about me, about the baby. I know that.

I hold little John and stare. He's heavy. My belly is heavy. Caty starts throwing the empty cans and trash into a cardboard box. With a folded up newspaper she sweeps cigarette butts onto another newspaper, tosses them into the box.

"Yikes!" she yells. "Someone pissed in a can. No wonder it stinks in here!"

She opens the window and tosses the can out.

"Fucking disgusting," she says. "We'll air this place out. I don't know how we'll survive here, but we will. We'll clean it out. I gotta call Ned. I gotta have a session."

Ned, Ned, Ned. She's always talking about Ned.

We hear footsteps, a dragging sound. It's Dau. He's dragged a mattress up from the street, up four flights of stairs.

"You can use this," he says. "I'll see if I can get you another one tomorrow. Man, I need a joint. I gotta get going."

"He's gorgeous," says Caty when Dau's gone. "Oh, I got a crush on him. Tomorrow I gotta see Ned. You stay with John while I go to my session. I'll get us a sheet tomorrow and maybe a towel."

We're at the end of New York. Beyond us is the East River. From the open front windows we can look down on Avenue D. A black woman pushes a baby carriage along a sidewalk, littered with papers and bottles. An old man calls out, selling pretzels from a cart. Two kids stroll up to him, and one tries to swipe a pretzel. The man chases them off. At night we hear people arguing, car horns honking, bottles breaking on the pavement. Outside, I see the city moving. Inside, I feel my baby moving. I'm scared. I don't want to think about it.

A few days later, Steve comes by to see Caty and John. He looks around and shakes his head. "This is a rat hole," he says. "You can't stay here."

Steve says there's an apartment upstairs above his coffee shop on East Tenth Street. We can stay in it if we clean it out. We follow Steve back to his neighborhood.

Caty leaves me in the coffee shop with John. She gets a bucket of water and a mop and goes to work. It takes hours to scrub off the layers of dirt and grime. We move in. It's a railroad flat. You have to walk through the bedrooms to get to the kitchen. The front room has high, embossed ceilings and a round arch. Someone has nailed some old muslin to the wall. Newspaper is tacked up over the side windows so people in the next building can't see in.

I hang out in the apartment. I wander from room to room, sometimes holding John, sometimes just staring. People come and go. Caty's friends. They smoke hash and talk and hang out. They spend the night, crash on the floor. One of Caty's friends stays for a few days, a Japanese woman named Yoko Ono. She's just left her husband and child. Caty knew her in Chicago. She doesn't speak. We both wander around the empty apartment. Even when we're in the same room, we don't speak. She wants to be alone in her thoughts.

After we've been living on East Tenth Street for about a week, Caty asks if I've seen a doctor. I tell her I haven't seen one since Portland, since the intern accused me of trying to abort.

"You have to see a doctor," she says.

"I don't have any money."

"Go to Bellevue. It's run by the city. They have to take you."

Caty puts me on a bus. I go uptown. Bellevue Hospital. Where the drug addicts and alcoholics go. I don't have any ID. No money either. They say I need ID, but it's a city hospital, so they take me.

I wait until a doctor examines me. Tests. The doctor tells me I have toxemia. He asks why I haven't seen anyone. He says the baby may be born dead. He says I should have taken better care of myself.

What did I know? I didn't know that I was going to have a baby. I don't know if I want to have a baby. But if I have a baby, I don't want it to be dead.

Toxemia. I've never heard of it. I find out it's because my thyroid was taken out when I was sixteen. The doctor sends me home and tells me to come back in a week.

I go back to East Tenth Street to our almost-empty apartment. I tell Caty. She says we have to read Adele Davis. We go the library a few blocks away and get Adele Davis' book, *Eat Healthy*. We find out Adele Davis had a thyroid condition. I learn that my immune system is weak. Since I don't have a thyroid, the baby isn't getting everything it needs. I learn that I need lecithin.

Caty has some money she's borrowed from someone. She goes out and buys a big bottle of lecithin, and she says, "Here—you have to take a tablespoon every few hours." I do. The lecithin granules are soft in my mouth. They have a buttery flavor. The taste is all right. I keep eating it.

MEETING NED

§

Ned. They keep telling me I have to meet Ned. Caty, Steve, Nancy, the others. He's a teacher, they say, a therapist. But he's more than that. He's not like other therapists and psychiatrists. He really believes that people can change. He has new ideas about how the mind works—ideas from Zen and other Eastern philosophies. They've never met anyone like him. He can help me, they say. I don't believe it. I don't want to see him. Caty has told me about him. He's a fat Jewish man, like one of my uncles.

Caty gets mad at me. "Well, he doesn't want to see you either," she says. "He's already got too many disturbed patients. He doesn't need another one. Besides, he's moving his practice to California and taking all his patients with him. Me included. I'm going to California with him. We're leaving. What are you going to do?"

I don't know what to say. I don't know what I'm going to do.

Caty picks up the phone, dials, talks.

"But what are we going to do with her?" she pleads. "She's almost eight months pregnant. We can't just leave her ..."

She hangs up the phone and looks at me as though she's just won a big argument.

"Friday morning," she says. "Ned will see you then."

Oh, God! What am I getting myself into? I've heard about how Ned tells people to explore their feelings instead of burying them. I've heard he's experimented with having patients take mescaline and LSD—like Timothy Leary and Richard Alpert. Only Ned isn't using those drugs now. He says there are other ways to explore the unconscious mind. It sounds crazy. I don't want to see him. Do I have to go through with this?

On Friday, I go to midtown Manhattan, Thirty-first Street. Eastside. It's hot and humid. I cross a busy street and walk up the steps of a three-story brownstone to the third floor. I open the door. A man's voice calls out, "I'll be there in a minute." Then I see him. Ned Adelsohn. Short, balding, fifties. He's wearing a white, short-sleeved shirt, blond chest hairs poking out at the open collar.

He comes right toward me. He looks like my uncles, except with a warm, wide smile and dancing eyes. A big Jewish Buddha.

He takes both of my hands in his and says he's glad to see me. He looks me right in the eyes. He looks at me as if he knows me, not trying to figure out what's wrong with me.

"Come in," he says.

I follow him into his office and sit. It's hot. A fan in the corner is blowing at me.

Ned sits back in an old wooden swivel chair and lights a cigarette. For a minute he just looks and smiles. His eyes are green. The fabric of his shirt is stretched tight where his belly hangs over the brown gabardine pants.

He asks question after question.

Where am I from? How many times was I in the hospital? Which hospitals? What happened there? When is the baby due? What do I want to do with the baby? Have I thought about adoption? What kind of jobs have I had?

Question after question in a calm, clear voice. Nodding his head as I answer. All the time looking at me as if he knows me, as if I'm not crazy.

He puts out his cigarette and rolls his chair closer to me. What does he want? For a moment I want to run, but I don't.

"You know we're going to San Francisco," he says.

"Yes."

"Would you like to come with us?"

I hesitate. I don't know what to say.

"I'd like you to come with us. Will you?"

I shrug.

"We'll be driving in a caravan. You won't be able to go by car. You'll have to fly."

I just stare and nod.

"Do you have any money?"

"No. I don't have anything, just this dress I'm wearing. And a car."

I tell Ned about the car Renee bought with the money she got my parents to send out. It's a VW bug. Brand new. I've never driven it. It's sitting there in Portland, Oregon.

Ned says he'll pay for my plane ticket, a one-way ticket to San Francisco. He'll try to sell the car when we get to the West Coast.

"I'm leaving in a few weeks," he says. "I'll need a week or so to get set up, and then you can join us. I'll pick you up at the airport."

I nod. I'm going to San Francisco.

Ned's holding my hands again and looking right at me, right into me, with his green eyes.

"It won't always be like this, Joan," he says. "You can have a life—a real life. But you'll need to do the work."

I'm confused. What kind of work? The room is hot and sticky, and I feel panic rising in my stomach.

He goes on. "Sometimes it will be tough, and you'll just have to hang in there. But if you do the work, things will be different."

I don't understand, but I nod.

"You need to think about the baby," he says. "Your life will probably be better if you give the baby up for adoption. But I'll respect whatever you decide to do. Go with your instincts. I trust your instincts."

Trust. Instincts. Travel. San Francisco. A real life. Getting better. Work. Doctors have never spoken to me like this before.

THE PARTY

※

Caty announces, "Some people from the Foundation are coming over. We're having a little get-together." The Foundation is what they call this group of people who are all Ned's patients.

I'm sitting on a kitchen stool. My legs dangling. My big belly getting bigger. People from the Foundation come in. It's a big room, high ceilings. It has a muslin curtain we put over the window. Furniture we dragged upstairs from the street.

"Hi, Joanie," I hear.

Estelle, a social worker from Brooklyn, Larry, a balding, red-haired Irish guy. People I've just met. Caty tells me to sit on the stool. I'm higher than the others. They're all sitting on the floor. A joint is passed around. I pass. I'm almost eight months pregnant.

Caty starts, "Joan, actually this party is for you."

"Me?"

"Yeah, we thought it's a good idea. We think you should think about the future, the baby. What are you going to do? How are you going to keep the baby? We want what's best for you."

"George, stand up," someone says.

George. He's an actor friend of Caty's. Dark hair, bulging muscles. He works out.

George stands up.

"Come on, George. Get next to her." He slowly walks toward me. He looks away.

Caty continues. "Now George here has agreed to marry you. Haven't you, George?"

"Sure."

"Well, put your arm around her."

"But …," I say.

"Yeah, we know George is gay. But he's agreed to marry you and go to California with us. We all think it's a good idea. That way you'll have a home for you and the baby. Right, George?"

He looks away.

The room starts spinning. I see bright yellow, orange colors coming at me. I want to run. What's going on?

"Now don't jump to conclusions," I hear. "Think about it."

I jump off the stool. I scream, "No!"

I bolt out the door, down the stairs onto the street. No shoes and a plaid dress that's too long for me. I run. It's late. I want to keep running. I'm getting out of breath. Marry George? Gay George? No, no, no. I want to be loved. No, George doesn't want to marry me. Let me out!

Larry comes after me, "You can't be on the street like this. Get inside."

Someone else comes. I scream. A police officer comes over with a stick. "What's going on here?"

"Oh, she's sick officer. She got a little confused. We're taking her home."

"Well, get going. Keep her off the streets."

They walk me back. I toss, I pull, I fight. Larry and some others hold my arms tight. I want to get away. I scream again. George puts his hand over my mouth. I won't stop. "No," I keep screaming. We get back to the apartment on East Tenth Street. I hear Caty on the phone.

"Yeah, she ran out of the building. We don't know what to do with her."

It's after midnight, more like two in the morning.

I hear Caty say, "He's coming over. Just hold her."

The party's over. I'm sitting in a corner holding my knees, rocking back and forth. Caty has left the apartment door standing open. He walks in carrying a black satchel. Ned Adelsohn. Ned, who's going to help me go to San Francisco. Ned who said someday it will be different.

He reaches down to me, takes my hand, says, "Can we sit down somewhere?" Caty shows him the bed in the middle room of the rail-road flat. He sits beside me. He asks what happened. I shake my head. I don't know what to say. He tells me it's okay to feel what I'm feeling.

"Joan," he says, "just hold on. I don't know what happened to you as a kid. You'll need to do the work. If you do that work, someday you'll have a life." He looks at me. He's not yelling at me.

I like Ned. He holds my hand. "Come to the office in the morning," he says. "Now, get some sleep." He goes to the front room, tells Caty I'm okay. Someday it will be different.

Hayes Street, San Francisco

৪

I board the plane with a note from the doctor at Bellevue Hospital that says I'm healthy enough to fly. I'm almost eight months pregnant. Never been to California. I hand the note at check-in. On the plane I stare straight ahead.

My eyes fill up.

What if the baby is born on the plane?

I should never have agreed to fly.

I sit on the long flight, wondering if the baby will be born on the plane.

What if it's born dead?

Ned is standing there when I get off the plane. I notice his smile, his hands. He takes hold of my hands with his larger but not large hands and says, "So glad you're here. It's the right thing. I'll take you to where you're staying."

I'm wearing my usual sleeveless smock dress. It was warm in New York. It's chilly here, not the California I thought I was going to. I need a sweater. Ned takes my small carry-on bag—we don't have to wait for luggage;I don't have any.

Ned takes me to a rooming house on Hayes Street near Golden Gate Park. The landlady with dyed red hair and fluffy blue slippers shows us to my room. Ned has made the arrangements. Harry, Ned's secretary, meets us there. Ned tells me that I'm on the second floor and Harry is on the first. I stare at Harry as he blows back the slick dark strands of hair falling down his face. He talks quickly, moves awkwardly, holds a bottle of beer in his hand, no matter what time of day.

I've never stayed in a rooming house; I've never even been in a rooming house. One bathroom on the floor to share with strange people I don't know. Renters in and out. My room has a sagging double bed in the center and an old hot plate on a low dresser to one side. Old bed, old dresser. Old, like my Grandma Fanny's apartment in the Bronx, where we visited and sat in the stuffed chairs with the drapes closed—inside on a sunny day—where I could hear the screams from Yankee Stadium.

The landlady shifts her feet in the blue fluffy slippers and says, "You can only stay here until the baby is born. I won't have a baby here in the house." Her voice gets louder. "I hope you understand no babies here in my house." Do I agree? I nod yes three times.

Ned pulls up a chair, swings it around, sits down with his legs wrapped around the sides, holding onto the chair back and facing me. "Get some rest," he says. "Harry, here's a few dollars. Please bring Joan something for dinner and show her around the neighborhood so she knows where the market is." Turning back to me, he says gently, "Call Harry if you need anything. I'll be back tomorrow."

MT. ZION

‰

Mt. Zion Hospital, the Jewish hospital. They'll have to take care of me. They take care of their own. The glass doors slide open, and I feel as if I'm in Newark, Beth Israel Hospital.

I walk in.

I wait.

People are walking back and forth.

People are rushing.

People are talking.

I sit there.

I see women with diamond rings and high-heel shoes.

I see men in suits and ties.

I go up to the lady at the desk. "I have an appointment. When will I be taken?"

"Sit down, miss. You'll have to wait your turn. Charity cases must wait. We're very busy here."

I want to scream, "Let me out. Let me out!"

I need to go to the bathroom. "Where's the bathroom?"

The lady points.

I walk and keep walking

I can't stay here.

I walk outside the revolving door. I walk to the side of the building. Pee comes down my leg. I hate this place. I won't keep my appointment. I won't have the baby here.

Children's Hospital

❦

I tell Ned on his daily visit that I can't go to Mt. Zion. "I can't." He asks the landlady in the blue fluffy slippers, "Where is the nearest hospital?" and she says, "Why, Children's Hospital. It's just down the street."

Ned calls. One hundred forty dollars—flat rate for having a baby. No charity. Just $140 I don't have. Ned hands me $140 in bills. "I'll sell the VW," he says. "I'll try to get to Portland this week. You're going to need the money."

Children's Hospital. I go into the waiting room. My eyes scan the room, and my body doesn't twitch, doesn't say, oh no. My body sits in the chair with maybe a dozen other women crowded into the room. Women with dark skin and dark hair, women with big stomachs, women with no lipstick, with washed smocks over their tight black skirts. Home. Maybe, not home, but I feel comfortable here.

I sit next to a woman with a protruding stomach, with a young child on her lap. "Now be a good girl," she says, in broken English. "Mama will be finished soon."

"Do you mind keeping an eye on her?" she says to me. "Just for a moment." I nod. The woman lifts herself out of the chair, walks to the ladies' room, and returns in a few minutes.

"Thank you," she says politely. "I can't carry her anymore." She looks at me. "First child?" she asks. I nod again. "Oh, don't worry," she says. "They get easier. This is my fourth." I hear a Spanish name, and she and the baby girl go with the nurse, the lady taking her daughter's hand.

I look around some more. All obviously pregnant women sitting, waiting, waiting for their names to be called. I hear "Miss Waldman." After the preliminaries and handing over the $140 cash, I meet the doctor, a tall handsome man with curly red hair. He smiles. He talks to me. He examines me. "Well, your file says you haven't seen a doctor recently. You're lucky. Everything appears normal."

Normal. Toxemia. Normal. The lecithin worked. Normal. I like this doctor. I like this hospital.

Private Adoption

§

Ned visits me every day in my room with the sagging double bed and yellow chenille bedspread and old hot plate. He asks me what I want to do about the baby. He talks to me about adoption. He says, "Joan, you have a lot of work to do. You'll have a much fuller life if you give the baby up for adoption." I tell him I tried to get into the Florence Crittenton Home for Unwed Mothers when I was still in Portland, but the social worker said I wouldn't fit because they only cater to teenage unwed mothers. I pull out the little piece of paper with the story about private adoptions that I cut out of a magazine when I was in Dammash in Oregon. I've been carrying it around all these months. I tell him I will call the number.

§

I waddle into the downtown San Francisco law office. The secretary ushers me into a big room with a long black table, straight-back chairs, and a floral-patterned sofa under the window. The lawyer comes in with a big smile and outstretched hand. "Miss Waldman," he says, "I'm so glad you could make it today. We're here to help you find a good home and family that will take good care of your baby and provide opportunities as the child grows up." He points for me to sit on the sofa. I sink into the soft cushions.

The secretary brings me a paper plate with cookies and asks if I would prefer coffee or tea. I don't want to eat here. I just want this over with. "Let me start by asking you a few questions," the lawyer with the big smile says. He wants to know where I'm from, my father's name, what he does for a living, my mother's name, the schools I went to, my jobs. He doesn't ask and I don't tell him about the two mental hospitals, the shock treatments, my father.

He asks about the baby's father. His name is Greg. We lived in the same house for eight months in Portland. I don't know if he's still there. He went to college—the University of Chicago. He was taken out of high school at sixteen to go to college, to a special program for bright kids. He didn't like it, so he dropped out and moved to the West Coast. He takes medicine for TB. I don't tell about the big scar up and down his wrist from when he tried to kill himself.

The lawyer tells me about the adoption process. It takes a year until it's final. Then he says, "Please make yourself comfortable. I'll be back in a few minutes."

When he's gone, I stare at the law books, shelf after shelf. I go to the bathroom several times. The lawyer and the secretary come back. Another lawyer, a woman, is with them. They pull up chairs next to the sofa and face me. The secretary takes out her note pad, and the woman lawyer takes over. "We think you'll be very happy with any of these three families," she says, pointing to the folders in her lap. I look at the first photo–a fifties ranch house with a big yard and a swing set. "A lot of room for the child to run around," the woman lawyer says. She talks about the beautiful house and tells me they are a good family from Texas—a loving Christian family with one adopted child and ready for another now. I can't believe this is happening to me. My baby going to a Christian family from Texas! No way! I sink back into the soft cushions on the floral-patterned sofa and feel trapped. I can't move.

I am able to say, "What else do you have? Do you have any intellectual people? Maybe a professor, maybe a couple with academic ties? Someone who cares about equal rights?"

"Ah, then you'll like this family," the woman lawyer says. The husband is a professor. He's from India. His wife is American. They have a big, lovely home just waiting to be shared with a child—but they can't have one of their own. Ann Arbor, Michigan is a great college town, interesting, intellectual."

I look at the faces of two smiling people standing in front of a big white house with dark blue shutters. The lawyer with the big smile chimes in, "Just look at the house! Perfect for a child to grow up in."

"That's a possibility," I say, going through the motions. Something isn't right. I can't give my baby to this family with a big house. Why do the lawyers have to talk about these big houses?

The woman lawyer moves on to the third family. "Let me introduce you to Mr. and Mrs. Cohen from Ohio." They're Jewish. They own a small grocery store. He shows me a brick house like the houses in West Orange, which is wealthier than Hillside where I grew up. My stomach churns. The baby kicks. I don't say anything, but I know. My father owns a grocery store. I can't let my baby live with people who own a grocery store.

I run out of the office, tears streaming down my face. I see a woman with a little girl. Will I look at every kid on the street and wonder if it is mine, the one I gave away?

Later, I'm sitting on my bed with the chenille bedspread back on Hayes Street, hugging my knees to my chest. I tell Ned the baby can't go to Mr. and Mrs. Cohen.

"Do you think you can take care of a baby?" I shake my head hard. No, no, no, I don't know what I want. I sob and sob some more and shake my head. Why is Ned trying to force me to have the baby adopted?

Ned is quiet. "Let me look into a few things," he says.

When he comes the next day, he tells me that welfare places the baby in a foster home for a month before adoption to make sure everything is in place. You have some time before making a permanent decision. Foster home for a month. Doesn't sound so bad. I tell Ned OK. I don't know what else to do.

My Belly Is Big Now:
Lying on the Grass

§

I walk down the stairs of the rooming house onto Hayes Street. It's late morning, and the sun is out, but I can still feel the chill of the air even though it's July. Not like July at home in New Jersey with the fans going, with "Let's get out of here and go swimming." Here, I don't feel that humid air. Here, I feel the breeze that takes me down the stairs and outside. I need to go to the supermarket. I've been walking almost every day to Safeway and getting a piece of liver to cook on the hot plate, walking down Fell Street on the Panhandle, the narrow strip of grass by Golden Gate Park. Today the sun is out. I turn at Ashbury and walk toward Haight Street. I'll go to Safeway later.

At the end of Haight Street, I cross Stanyon. Golden Gate Park. I look up. Sun, real sun in San Francisco. Guys with long hair, women with long hair and long skirts. My belly is big now. A pregnant woman coming the other way smiles at me and nods. I smile back, the smile of a knowing woman, the smile of belonging. I love that feeling. I lie down, tuck the ends of my dress under me and look around. There's no one nearby. Just me and my belly and me and the grass underneath. I feel high, but I'm not. Just me and the baby, kicking, feeling the baby kicking. Really kicking.

I don't think about Ned telling me I should consider adoption. I don't think about not having any place to live, about not having any money. I don't think about anything else. Just this moment. I am here lying on the grass in Golden Gate Park. Alone with my thoughts. Usually, I don't know where I am. I look out and see the streets of Newark, the streets of Portland. But this moment, I do know. I'm in Golden Gate Park at the end of Stanyon Street on the grass by myself. No one around me, and I can feel the sun coming down, and I can feel the life in me.

WAITING

℘

Waiting, waiting in the rooming house on Hayes Street, waiting for the baby to be born. My baby that's going to a foster home. I don't think about it. I just think about walking up and down the hall. Waiting, going to the bathroom, taking my vitamins. I don't think about being alone, being lonely, crying out inside, "What's wrong with me? Why don't I have a home? Why don't I have a husband?"

I'm in the room watching the minutes tick by. The landlady knocks on my door. "You got visitors," she says. The door opens late at night, and there's Caty in her Zorrie flip-flops, Steve behind her, and little John asleep on his father's shoulder.

"Oh, we're so glad we found you," she blurts out. "We just got in. It's been a long trip. The car broke down in Iowa. How are you?"

Her voice, her familiar voice. I hear her nonstop questions, nonstop sentences. The room is filled with people, with sounds. "Are you okay?" Caty rambles on. She doesn't wait for an answer. It's so good to see her, hear her. I don't feel so alone. I want to hug her, but my stomach is between us, and Caty doesn't like to hug. Neither do I. It doesn't matter. She's here. Caty is here. She rambles on more. I listen. I don't listen. "How's Ned? What's happening? Have you been to the Foundation yet? When are you due? How have you been getting along?"

I can't keep track. I hear Steve say, "Come on, Caty, we gotta go. We gotta get someplace to sleep." He taps her thin shoulder. She gives me a quick sideways squeeze. "We'll see you. I'll come by soon. Promise."

The door closes. The noise stops. The room is quiet again. I can hear the sounds of the hallway, the quiet rasping cough from a room, the creaking door. An hour later, maybe two, my stomach hurts. I have to go to the bathroom. This time I know I have to go to the bathroom. I walk down the hallway. I sit on the toilet—all of me, and I can't go. Oh, I have to go. I walk back. Take the vitamins that Adele Davis says eases labor, eases pain. I don't know what to do. Maybe, I'm in false labor. Maybe, I should go to the hospital. I waddle back to the room. My stomach hurts. I don't want to be alone. I don't want to stay here anymore. I don't want to call Harry. I'll go to the hospital. I've heard that with the first baby you have false labor. I'm in false labor.

Knock on the landlady's door.

"What you want?" I hear through the door.

"Can you call a cab for me?"

"Okay. Go upstairs, and I'll tell you when it's here."

I waddle upstairs, sit on the edge of the bed with my packed bag that I've had packed for a week—a toothbrush, a nightgown, socks, deodorant. Knock on the door.

"He's here."

I have a hard time walking down the stairs. The landlady holds my arm, and it's easier. The taxi driver sees me and says, "Where to, lady?"

"Children's Hospital."

REUVEN'S BIRTH

&

"Hey lady," I hear from an orderly in a green uniform, "you're going to have a baby. No time to prep you. Why didn't you come in sooner?" I want to say I thought I was in false labor, but I can't. My body takes over. My stomach hurts, my insides hurt, I hurt. I stare straight ahead. I'm on a gurney downstairs in the emergency room with the orderly beside me and the curtain drawn around. He says, again, "No time to prep you. We gotta get you upstairs."

A nurse comes in and asks if I want a spinal. I don't know what a spinal is. She says, "We just give you an injection. It will numb you from the waist down. You'll be awake. You can even watch the birth. The nurse looks as if she knows what she's talking about. My body is heaving. I nod. After the needle goes in, I can hear the click-clack of the wheels as I am taken upstairs. The moving pain stops. Everything stops. What's happening? Nothing. I can't feel. I'm put on a bigger table by myself, and I see my handsome doctor standing over me. A big table, my doctor all scrubbed, holding his hands out, lights above me.

My doctor asks if I want to see the baby being born. He points to the mirror above. "You'll be able to watch." I nod. He swings the mirror over my head and shows me the angle from which to watch. I look but no feeling. I want my feeling back. I want my stomach convulsing. I want to feel the baby coming out. Nothing. But I watch.

I see gush. Oh! It's coming out. Oh, it's horribly deformed! Oh, I'm a failure. Oh, what will I do? I have a deformed baby.

The doctor speaks. "I wish they were all this easy. You have a boy."

"Is he okay?" I mumble from the table.

"As healthy as they come. He'll be cleaned up soon."

Afterbirth. Not deformed. Why don't I know these simple things?

The baby is covered and put on top of me on the narrow, high table where I lie strapped in the recovery room. Movement all around, back and forth, patients screaming, "Nurse, nurse." I stay still. Alone. Alone with my baby on a narrow gurney. My body screams no. I lie there silent. The baby. I stare down at the baby. I don't feel anything. No joy. No tears. Nothing. Just numb. Numb as my insides, which just delivered a healthy seven-pound, three-ounce boy. *My legs hurt. Why are they so stiff? My legs hurt badly. Sounds above me. All alone. I faint.*

I open my eyes. I'm in the ward. A nurse—an old nurse dressed in white—stands over me.

"Here's your baby. He can stay with you for an hour. Here's the bottle. You can start feeding him."

Feed him. How do I do that? Adele Davis, the guru for healthy babies says to breastfeed. Especially the first three days so the milky white substance, colostrum, can come in. It provides immunities for life. I'll breastfeed my baby. At least I can give him that much. I put my breast close to his little mouth. He won't take the nipple. I must be doing something wrong. He won't suck. Oh, he's going to die.

Help! It's so dark in here. Midnight. Overhead lights. My mind follows the lights. I don't know where I am. Lights overhead. Silent voices over me. Bad girl. You shouldn't have gone down there.

Mad thoughts come in and out. A new nurse comes in. A pretty nurse with a white starched dress. Pretty hands, pretty eyes, kind eyes.

"Miss Waldman, why are you breastfeeding your baby? Welfare is picking him up on Friday. He's being put up for adoption in a month."

I explain about Adele Davis and colostrum. She comes closer to me and draws the curtain around. So close. *What did I do wrong?*

"Listen," she says in a firm and soothing voice. She pulls the curtain closed. "Listen to me. Take your baby out of here. Once you sign the welfare papers from the hospital, it's almost impossible to get him back. Take him home."

Home. I have no home. I'm staying in a furnished room in Haight-Ashbury. There are no babies allowed in the boarding house. Home, where is my home? Where can I bring a newborn baby? I tell her I don't have a home, don't know how to diaper a baby, don't have any clothes for him. I can't take care of a baby.

"Come with me," the nurse in the white starched dress says to me.

I follow her, through the ward, down the long corridor smelling of Lysol, to a small room, a room full of dolls and diapers and pins. She announces, "We are going to learn how to diaper a baby."

"I can't, I can't, I can't!" I wail.

"Pay attention," the kind nurse says.

Attention, pay attention to what? Where am I?

"Now, you fold the diaper in thirds with the open edge toward you. Put the doll on top. Now, we hold the end overlapped and pin each side."

"I can't, I can't, I can't."

"You can."

Over and over, we fold, put the doll on top and pin. Minutes, hours, much later I can diaper the doll. The kind nurse with the starched white uniform walks me back through the long corridor to my ward. She stands by my side and announces to the other ladies in my room, "Miss Waldman is going to keep her baby. Can each of you donate a piece of clothing from your layettes?"

She goes around to each bed on the ward and collects an article of clothing, nightshirts, receiving blanket, and a blue fleece bunting. Everything I need, except diapers.

"Now," she says as she helps me crawl back into my hospital bed, "you need to leave before Friday, before the welfare comes. You must leave on Thursday."

"But, I have no place to go." No place.

"Isn't there someone who can help you?"

"Ned, my therapist."

I call him on the pay phone in the hall. "The nurse wants me to leave on Thursday." The nurse speaks to Ned and explains the situation. Then she gives the phone back to me.

Ned says, "Joan, the nurse tells me it might be better not to sign any papers at the hospital. Are you thinking you might want to keep the baby?"

"I don't know what I want."

"Well, whatever you decide, I'll support you. You know that."

"Okay. What should I do?"

"I'll pick you up on Thursday, and I'll look for a place where you can stay."

"But I don't have any diapers."

Ned says he will bring some diapers when he picks me up on Thursday.

PART 3

&

DIVING DEEP

REUVEN, FIRST NIGHT HOME

ॐ

August 1965. On Thursday, Ned comes to the hospital with a package of Pampers, the new disposable diapers, and a white bassinet from Goodwill. As we walk out, Ned stops right outside the door. I look at him. Is something wrong? He puts his arms out. I see that he wants to hold the baby. He uncovers the tiny head from the receiving blanket. Standing, holding the baby, he says, "I feel like a grandfather."

Before I went into the hospital, Ned had assured me he would find a place for me to stay. He always does what he says he will do. He got me the ticket to San Francisco; he went up to Portland to sell my VW Bug. I've never known anyone that I could trust the way I trust him. We get in the car. "I couldn't find a place," he apologizes. "I called around, but there doesn't seem to be anyplace that will take a newborn. I talked to Sue, and she said you can spend the night in the place where she's staying on Derby Street in Berkeley, but she's moving out tomorrow." Sue's an artist who is also in the Foundation. We spent a lot of time together in New York before we came out to San Francisco.

Just one night. Oh my gosh, I say to myself, "How can he do this to me? I won't have anyplace to stay. What am I going to do? Oh, why did I listen to Ned? Oh, I won't find anyplace to stay. How can I?"

We walk into an old two-story house. Holding the baby tight, I open my eyes to beer bottles, cigarette butts, musty smells, ripped chairs, glaring lights overhead. Sue is there with her nine-year-old daughter, Betsy. I don't know what to say. My face, my eyes, my shoulders slump. I ask where I can put the six pack of milk the hospital has given me, and Sue points to the kitchen. I put it in the fridge. I open the door and the smell hits me. Rotten, rotten, rotten.

I stare ahead as Sue takes me upstairs to rooms that are empty except for stained mattresses on the floor. Sue and Betsy take one bedroom. Sue points to the other. She puts a torn sheet on the bed and then a torn blanket. "This will have to do," she says. They take turns holding the baby and cooing to him. We all take turns saying goodnight.

I shut the door. Alone with the baby in a blue bunting from another mother on the ward. I stare at him. He moves. I don't know what to do. I don't change clothes, I don't wash. I just lie down and put the baby besides me. I put my arm out and put him in the crook of my arm. Then I hold my breath and wait. I don't know what I'm waiting for. Will he survive the night? When should I feed him? The mattress is under a window. It's open, and I can feel a breeze coming through. I want to sleep but I can't. I look at the baby. He moves his mouth. I try to give him my breast, but he doesn't grab on so I just stare. The air is cool. I feel as if it's blowing right through me. Oh, he's going to die. Oh, God help me. There's a little light from the moon, but it's night and it's dark. I hold my breath. I let go. I stare at the baby's face. I feel a little movement, tiny breaths. Is he going to die? I watch. I wait. Nothing changes. I don't move. I don't dare move. I don't want him to die.

Suddenly I hear a loud wail in the night. I run into the hall with the baby. Betsy and Sue are there. Sue says, "It'll be okay. Betsy just got scared." Silently we go back to our respective bedrooms, feeling the isolation of the night, feeling the strangeness of this life.

I take the baby back to the mattress on the floor, lie down, and wait. As I lie there, the night slowly, very slowly ticks by. I can feel each moment. Then I look up, and I see light coming through, not the moon but the sun. I look at the baby, and he's asleep, but I can see his mouth moving, I can feel him breathing. I wait some more. More light. Light on his face. As I watch the sun come up, as I watch the baby's breath, as I watch the light come through the window, I breathe a little deeper. I hold the baby tight. I don't know how I know, but I know he's breathing, he's alive. I know somehow down deep that we're going to make it.

In the morning, Sue and Betsy go out, and I'm left alone in the big damp house with the baby. I try nursing him, but he can't figure out how to hold onto my nipple. I decide to give him the bottle the nurses at the hospital gave me in the six-pack to take home. I remember my mother, when my brother was a baby, turning the bottle upside down to make sure enough milk flows out. When I do that, nothing happens. I also remember hearing somewhere that I can prick the nipple with a needle, but the needle needs to be sterilized. I put a match to a needle and prick the nipple with it. Still nothing happens. I begin to panic. My baby will die. I will never be able to feed him. I'm alone in the dark, damp rambling house on Derby Street. There's no telephone. I keep stabbing the nipple, making bigger and bigger holes and still nothing happens.

Just then the doorbell rings. It's a large black woman—a realtor has sent her because the house is for rent. I burst into tears. I tell her my saga. She takes the bottle and turns it upside down. Again, no milk. Then she calmly unscrews the nipple, takes out a black plastic piece inside, screws the nipple back on, and the milk pours out.

I want to die. How am I going to take care of a baby when I don't know the simplest things like unscrewing the nipple? The baby, who by this time is very hungry, grabs the nipple and sucks eagerly.

STAYING IN BERKELEY

&

Sue has a friend named Clarence, a large black man who is friendly with most of the hippies in the area, probably supplying them with dope. He comes over, takes one look at the situation, and says, "Girl, we have to get you out of here." He comes back later, says he found a place for me, helps me pack our few belongings, and drives me cross-town to the black section of Berkeley to stay with a woman he knows there.

He takes me to a white, single-family house with a small porch and a large front yard full of parched grass. We walk up the steps to the house, and an elderly black lady wearing bright green slippers and a faded housedress answers the door. Clarence says this is Mrs. Johnson, but I can call her Bertha.

The house is neat and orderly. There are doilies and bric-a-bracs all around. The air smells as if the overstuffed furniture has been there forever. There's nothing familiar. I want to go home, but I have no home. Bertha says I can stay for a week or two and the fee will be twenty dollars a week. I look at Clarence. I have no money. He takes out twenty dollars and pays the woman. He never says a word to me. Wow! I've never known anyone who would do that.

Bertha moves about casually in her faded housedress and slippers, shows me my room. It's a small room right off the kitchen with a double bed pushed up against an oversized dresser. She tells me to unpack my things and take care of the baby. Although I've officially named him Reuven, I can't call him anything yet. He isn't Reuven; he isn't a person to me. So I call him baby. I get into bed and again try nursing. He wails, his tiny face scrunching up.

Bertha comes in, sees me struggling and says, "Get closer, girl. Get closer so he can feel you." I do as she says, and the baby grabs onto my nipple. Success. Bertha tells me, "You need to relax and let me take care of things. Just get some rest and feed your baby. Hear me?"

I lie in the bed for most of the week. Bertha does our wash. She feeds me. Just having the freedom to lie in bed and pay attention to the baby, I feel my system beginning to calm down, and the milk starts to flow. Generally, Bertha leaves me alone in the room.

The radio is on almost all the time. I hear Bob Dylan singing, "Like a rolling stone ..." It's August. It's hot outside and inside. Music, words drift over me.

Then a news flash! The National Guard is coming. The National Guard is here. I stand up, go to the porch. I can hear noise outside. Bertha mumbles something about Watts burning. I don't know what Watts is—I just know I'm here with Bertha in a black neighborhood.

All of a sudden, the sky gets dark. They're coming to get me. I want to run, run away. I can't stand it. I know they're coming after me. I'm lost. It's dark down here. I see a man coming down the stairs to get me. I stare. It's cold. What's going to happen? I want to scream. Someone save me!

Bertha says, "Get inside. We'll be safe inside." I follow her.

Inside, I go back to my room. Bertha goes back to the kitchen, goes back to her cooking, doesn't pay attention to what's happening outside. The house is quiet. Bertha says we'll be all right. I believe her. No one's going to hurt us.

The next week, Clarence tells me that Sue has moved into an apartment on San Pablo Avenue, above Rose's Café, a Chinese restaurant. She says I can stay with her. Clarence again comes to move me.

TELEGRAPH AVENUE

&

There I am walking up this street, Telegraph Avenue, walking up to a place of high energy, of guys with long hair, tie-dye shirts, and sandals, smoking weed. No one pays attention to me. How can I get someone to look at me? Hot pink skirts, slinky girls with low cut blouses looking, looking at the boys, boys looking, looking around puffing, everyone puffing, holding, holding books, Lawrence Ferlingetti, standing, sitting, sitting outside Cody's sipping coffee, puffing weed.

I keep walking, the baby tied to my front, my fat belly sticking out, my insides wanting to spill all over the street, and I keep walking until the baby won't stop crying and I see his pursed mouth and I sit down on a chair in front of Cody's bookstore and I lift my Mexican blouse, my white blouse with stitched embroidery criss-crossed. The baby sucks, and I'm wondering what is going on as I can see people moving, and my feet want to move, and the baby is attached to my tit, and I want to scream, but I let him suck until I can't stand it anymore, and I lift him up, burp him, and start walking up the street, the only person with a baby, with a kid.

Everyone is walking fast, and my body is weighted down, and I keep going until I get to the edge of the campus, and there are boxes and a boy with no shirt and a beard and bushy hair screaming, "Down with the pigs. Get out now." Someone hands me a pamphlet. There's another box with another pamphlet about end the war now. Students are walking to the center by the fountain, the center called Sproul Hall, where there is a big crowd, and I look up and see two people on a platform, and a guy with dark hair is shouting, "Freedom now! What do we want? Freedom now!" A girl with long blond hair is shouting something about freedom, and I ask a guy next to me wearing a turtleneck sweater what's going on, and he says, "It's the Free Speech Movement, the administration is pigs—we're for freedom, freedom, lady, so that baby there can be free. Hear me, lady, freedom!"

I can't stand the noise, and the baby is screaming, and he's wet—I can feel it—so I duck through the crowd, and I walk away down Telegraph Avenue, and I stop now on the other side of the street and go into the bathroom in a café. I go in and unstrap the baby and start to change his diaper by the sink, and a girl comes out and blows smoke in my face and says, "Cool, lady, cool." I want to go home, so I get the diaper changed, and I walk down Telegraph Avenue to the green and white sign that crosses Dwight Way and walk down Dwight Way into the apartment above the restaurant, and my face is wet. Tears are coming down, and I don't know what is going on. I call Ned, but he's in session. Harry says he'll call me back, and I lie on the mattress on the floor, and the baby lies there with me, and Sue comes in and says, "Haven't you fed him?"

NED WANTS ME TO START PUTTING A LIFE TOGETHER

⅋

October 1965. Ned calls and tells me he wants to come out to Berkeley on Wednesday. We set a time. The room in Sue's apartment on San Pablo Avenue is empty except for the two wooden chairs we found outside. He pulls his chair close to me. He sits with the back of the chair facing me and his legs over the sides. "How are you doing? How are you managing with the baby?" He smiles.

He says, "It would be good for us to talk a little about your future." I listen. I don't know what he's talking about. I like sitting next to him, this big man next to me. "Joan," he says, "you're going to need to get a job. You're going to need to find a babysitter. You're going to need to come into San Francisco for therapy. I inquired about welfare, and you can't get it here in California. You need a year's residency. Your parents told me they would send money, but they haven't. You're going to need to get a job."

"No one is going to hire me," I tell him. I can't be a social worker. I don't know how to keep a job now. I can't work. I thought my parents would send money. What am I going to do? I say, "Maybe, I should call my father."

"No, Joan, I don't want you to have any contact with your parents. For a while. You need to make it on your own. We can have sessions about you getting a job, but you can't call your parents. Okay?"

"Okay."

"Talk to some of the others—Larry, Paul, Sandy—everyone's looking for a job. It would be good if you talk to the others. You're with people who care about you. You and Reuven can think of us as your family. We've all moved out here to create a community together. I know you can take care of yourself and the baby. You need to come into San Francisco and start doing the *work*. We'll try to set up something so you can bring Reuven in with you."

I nod.

"We'll take it step by step. First you find out about a job you can do. Then we'll deal with finding a babysitter. It's important for you to get a job, to take care of yourself and the baby. This is an important step. It's part of the *work* I've been talking about."

I don't understand, but I nod anyway.

"I've got to go soon. I'd like you to come in to San Francisco on Friday. I'm starting to give lectures on Friday nights. It will be good for you to be around other people from the Foundation. Now, just hold on. I know someday it will be different. For now, you need to do the *work*. I've got to leave now, but I'll see you Friday. Call me if something happens that you can't make it. Okay?"

I stare at the door as he leaves the apartment, walking down the rickety stairs to his black car parked in the back.

First Session at the Foundation
℘

November 1965. I take the Alameda County bus to San Francisco. Reuven is in front of me, a few months old, tied to my front in a striped muslin carrier. In San Francisco, we take the #22 Fillmore up the street to the new headquarters Ned has rented for the Foundation. I walk up a narrow stairway to a big room at the top. Everyone in the Foundation is gathering for Friday-night lecture. Almost everyone has arrived from New York by now. Betty, Estelle, others want to see the baby.

We gather in the room, the big room with people sitting in chairs in a circle. Others sit on the floor in front. Ned, his smiling Buddha self in a big chair, his elbows resting easily as he talks, as he welcomes everyone, as he says we need to do the *work*, go through the pain, we'll come out the other side but we need to go through the pain. It's inside anyway, he says and that's why this office has padded cells—he points to the hallway. On either side is a padded cell. You need to stoop down to get in. Get in and then let your feelings go, feel, scream, cry, pound, whatever you like—just don't hurt anyone. Do what your mother wouldn't let you do. We're here to do *work*, he says again. You need to do the *work*. We all feel bad about ourselves, but you don't have to go on living like this.

I'm holding Reuven.

I'm sitting on one of the folding chairs.

I don't hear what he's talking about. I do hear.

I start to nurse. I pick up my Mexican blouse.

Ned talks about new life, starting life, birth, the purity of new life and what happens.

We're going to have these meetings every Friday night. Other times—groups and private sessions. "I'm here to *work* with you."

The meeting is over.

I stand up. Other people come over to see the baby.

The baby. I want to crawl away. I want to run out of here. I can't stand it now. I start shuffling. *I start screaming. The voices coming out of me. The voices sitting in me. My mother screaming, "You're no good. No one wants you."* Me, carrying a baby, holding him next to me.

A body shocked.

A body trying to go through the motions of living.

A newborn baby, me in San Francisco, so far from where I grew up, far from Hillside, New Jersey, far from my high school friends.

How did it happen to me, sitting in this room on upper Fillmore? There is nothing in me that has prepared me for this. New Jersey, my girlfriends know to buy a house, have babies. Me, I walk up the stairs staring ahead, hearing you need to go through the pain. You need to come to consciousness. You need …

My body fights.

My mind fights.

My insides whisper, let me out, let me out.

Tomorrow, Ned says, we'll go into the padded cell—we'll begin the *work*.

How did I get here? I want to go home. Home. Where? I hear talk. I hear talk about apartments, moving, decorating, parties, life.

I stand there.

Someone takes the baby. "Can I hold him?"

Oh, sure, take the baby.

She holds the baby.

She looks at him.

She pinches his cheek.

What do I do?

I hold the baby, my hands stiff, my body stiff. I don't look at the baby. Diapers, formulas, babies. This is not supposed to happen. I should be in New York, working, big, small New York. I want to go to the Village. I want to be a beat writer, poet in the Village. How did this happen?

I scream, let me out. I want to go home. Ned, I don't want to do this. Let me out.

Ned talks to me. "You're free to go. You don't have to stay, but I think you'll come through if you do. Just hold on. It'll be okay." Words.

Caty says, "We'll give you a ride to the East Bay Terminal." Okay. On the bus, Reuven sleeps. My insides are talking. *What's going to happen to me? I've got to get out of here. Oh, God, help me.*

I keep talking to myself until I hear Berkeley, San Pablo Avenue. I get off, cross the street and walk up the stairs to the apartment above Rose's Café.

KEEP YOUR HAND MOVING

ℰ

December 1965. I'm alone with the baby. Sue's at work. Betsy's in school. I passed the test. I'm going to work as a Christmas temp at the Berkeley Post Office—swing shift, four to midnight. I call the babysitter whose number I found on the bulletin board at the Laundromat. She knows how to take care of kids, and she needs the money because her husband just split. We make an agreement.

I get the notice. Report to work on Monday. I'm excited. I call the babysitter back. "I'm so glad you're going to take care of my baby!"

"I can't do it," she tells me. "My husband won't let me. We just got back together."

I beg her, "Please, just for one night. Just until I can find someone else." But she hangs up on me.

Clarence stops by. He lumbers up the rickety stairs. "Hey, sister, what's happening here? Want a toke?"

"Clarence," I stammer, as I pace back and forth, "It won't work." I tell him the whole story.

"Sit down, girl," he says as he pulls on his suspenders and pulls up an old wooden chair. "Hold on. I know a lady down the street. Go down there now and tell her I sent you. It's that big white house in the middle of the block."

"Oh, Clarence, thanks." A hug. "You're really a life saver."

I put a sweater on the baby, strap him to my front, throw a bottle in the bag and go down the block to the big white clapboard house below San Pablo Avenue. A lady in a tight black halter and black tights comes to the door. She's got bright red lipstick on and grease on her hair. Her skin is dark bronze. We stand on the porch. "Clarence sent me. I need someone to watch my baby. I'm on the swing shift. Please can you do it?"

"Sure, lady, twenty-five dollars a week. When ya wanna start?"

"Tomorrow afternoon. Three o'clock."

"Bring some diapers and some bottles."

"Great. Thanks."

The next afternoon I leave the baby with diapers, bottles, a change of clothing, and even a baby carriage. I don't like pushing a baby carriage, but coming home at midnight, I can put all the stuff in the carriage and none on my back. This time the lady answers in a hot pink halter top and a short, spandex mini-skirt. There's loud music going, real loud. I don't care. I want to get to work, and I'm really glad to have a babysitter. I hand him over and say, "I'll be back after midnight. I look at him for a second in his bunting. He's quiet. I leave. No kiss. No hug. No pat on the head. I just leave.

I walk in at three fifty for the swing shift at the Berkeley Post Office. A big room. A big room with machines working, clacking and clinking. My supervisor, Mr. G. with a green bowtie and a short sleeved white shirt and a big belly calls me over and says, "Waldman, you come here."

I follow him to the clanging of machines. I follow him to a row of boxes, other employees, other hippies sitting on stools. "Here," he says, "you take the Bs. See Barstow, Berkeley, Burbank. Just sort by city and keep your hand moving. Hear me? Keep your hand moving."

I sit down and start sorting. I see mail being dropped into clanging machines. The machines spit out the mail, spit it out so that I can't stand the noise. I stare at the mail going down the chute. A buzzer rings loud and then louder. Mr. G. screams, "Break. All right, everyone take your break." Everyone stops working. I see a few people go behind sacks of mail. I smell that smell, the smell of dope, the smell of Telegraph Avenue, the smell of Berkeley.

Outside the bathroom, I see a guy with red bushy hair in a bright turquoise skirt and a tie-dye shirt sitting on the mail sacks. He calls a girl in a long madras dress, who is on my line, "Hey, babe, sit over here." He whips out a joint, and she takes a long drag. I head straight for the bathroom, take out the pump La Leche League has given me, and I pump. I finish, put the pumped milk in my bag, go out, and walk past the others. Why doesn't anyone want to sit next to me? I don't smoke dope. I don't make eyes at the guys. What is wrong with me?

Back at my station, the buzzer rings again, and the conveyer belt starts again, and I see boxes going down below to the basement of the post office, and I get dizzy. Where am I? I start crying, sobbing. My hand stops. Mr. G. passes in back of my stool and from behind I hear, "Waldman, I don't care what you do in here. Just keep your hand moving. Got that?"

I pick up the mail and start sorting again. I hear voices coming at me. I hear voices, *Push it over; get it in.* I hear voices, "It's stuck; get maintenance." I stand up. I sit down. I look up. I look down. I look up. It's dark in here, but the florescent lights are bright. The buzzer rings. Shift's over.

I go back to the babysitter's house. I open the unlocked door to a smoke-filled room, to very dim lights and couples dancing, shifting along, slowly, not paying attention to the loud music and to songs I've never heard before. A tall, dark-skinned man points upstairs, and I pick my way through the crowd to get to the baby upstairs. He's lying there buried in a bed filled with jackets, laundry, hash pipes, high-heeled shoes. Just the bed, chair, and no other furniture. I scoop him up and put him in the carriage and walk back to Sue's on Dwight Way. It's almost one in the morning. This schedule is going to be grueling. Mr. G. says we're going to work our asses off until after Christmas. I don't know how I am going to do this. I don't. I go to change the baby's diaper. He's soaked, and I see red spots. I've read that kids get red spots on their behinds. I just want to get to bed.

The next night and the next. The routine continues. Leave baby off. Get to post office by 3:55 p.m. The machines are going. The sorter. Again, I stand up. I sit down. I look up. I look down. I look up.

Snakes are crawling up the wall.

The wall is falling down.
Where am I?
I look at my body—snakes are crawling all over me.
Mr. G. comes by.
His head is two heads.
He has two heads!
Early morning the machines are going.
The snakes are climbing all over.
I can't stand looking out.
I want to get out of here.
I try walking.
A hippie guy comes toward me.
He's going to smash me.
I can see it in his eyes.
He walks by me, doesn't say anything.
I sit down again.
I get my mail and start sorting the *B*s until the snakes start coming at me again
They're all over.
I see them on the machine.
Small curly snakes.
Grey white snakes.
Curling around my body, squeezing tight.
Mr. G.'s heads talk. Each one is saying something.
I can't hear. I just want to get out of here.
I need some air.
I stand up.
Mr. G.'s heads walk by.
"Waldman," they say in unison, "keep your hand moving."
The buzzer rings.
Break.
I stand up.
I'm swaying. *I see everyone's got two heads now. All the hippies, all the supervisors. Two heads. What's happening?*
The buzzer rings again. Back to work. *My ears smash against the green wall, my ears catch the snakes, my ears hear ring, ring, ring. I look*

at the clock. Let me out, let me out. I close my eyes, walk back to my station, and the room is straightened out; it's stopped spinning. I sit down and start sorting the mail. No one notices. No one knows. I do. I've been here before. I know. The machines going, the people talking, the people moving around. The people—the hippies, the supervisors.

I look out.

Men screaming over here.

Move it over there.

Men walking with boxes.

Big boxes on their shoulders.

Little boxes in their arms.

Men moving.

Women moving.

People yelling back and forth.

Big machines moving.

My daddy's hand moving.

I stand quietly.

There must be a way to get out of here. The room is shaking, swaying. Where are the lights? Spray it on. Spray the water. Fire, fire, I hear. Get the fire out. No fire. Fire in my heart, fire burns out. My heart burns out.

I show up. There is no place to go. No place. Yet, I get there to the post office, and I pump my milk, and I stand there as the walls cave in, the snakes climb out, wanting to breathe the fresh air. But there is no fresh air here. It's just the old stale air. I wait for the last buzzer to ring.

No snakes tonight. No double heads. Just sorting mail, pumping milk, and pretending not to be interested in the guys who are hitting on the girls. When I go to pick up the baby on the third night, the tall dark-skinned man who is always nice to me is standing at the door. "Lady, you better take your baby out of here. The lady supposed to be taking care of him was picked up for prostitution three days ago. No one has been taking care of him."

No one taking care of him. Lying there. Diapers not changed. I look. His diapers are there the way I left them. I look. His milk is there the way I left it. How could it be? I look. His bottom is red. This time real red and swollen. He's howling. I'm howling inside. What am I going to do? God, if there is a God, please hear me. What is wrong with me? How come I don't notice these things? How come? I grab the baby and leave, pushing the carriage from the big white house off San Pablo Avenue.

Nowhere to go.

I can't quit. What am I going to do? Ned says I have to have a job. I can't get welfare. Need a year's residency. What, what should I do? Where am I going to find a babysitter by tomorrow? Where? It's hopeless. I'm hopeless. I walk and walk, cross the street. I look up and in the black night. I see a big brown house in front of me. I see a yellow and brown madras curtain across the front bay window. Madras. Hippie. It's a hippie house. I wipe the tears from my face and knock on the door. It's almost one a.m, but there's a light on. A tall woman smoking a joint answers.

"Lady, you're going to think I'm crazy, but I need to find a babysitter for my son." I open up the bunting and show her his face. "Do you know anyone in the area who could do it? I'm working at the post office."

"Oh, groovy, my husband just left. I need money. I'll do it."

Moving Metal, Shifting Shapes

ॐ

Spring 1966. Welding. I first hear the word from Robert, my next-door neighbor on San Pablo Avenue. New baby. No job. No money. No husband. I pick up stuff on the street, a cardboard box for a coffee table, a mattress for my bed. I see two bicycle wheels. I carry them upstairs with the baby on my back. I look at them. I want to pull the wheels apart. I want to twist them, bend them. I want to dig in there and make my hands move the metal. I want a different shape than the round rim, the symmetrical spokes. I want to move what's inside—the chaos, the crying out, the burning inside me. I want to move what I can't. I am the steel—hardened on the outside. I need to break open. I thought I could do it with my hands. They don't move, no matter how hard I try. I bring the bicycle wheels to Robert, who supplies dope and who rides a motorcycle.

"Oh, you have to cut and weld them," he says.

"What's that?"

"Welding—putting metal together. Can't do it with bare hands. You need a torch. You need equipment."

"Welding?" I say.

"It's called welding," he says again.

I know I have to learn to weld.

MEETING EFFIE

꙳

June 1966. I move from Berkeley to Hayes Street, San Francisco, the Fillmore. I transfer to Rincon Annex, the San Francisco Post Office. I start work Monday. I need to find a babysitter.

We meet Effie on the #22 bus going down Fillmore Street. She starts tickling Reuven's feet and says to me, "Girl, he should have socks on. He needs his feet covered."

She's friendly. She looks like she knows about kids. She tells me she took care of a white boy for two years. I don't like babies wearing socks, but I'm desperate.

"Can you take care of my baby? I need to go to work."

We make arrangements. She lives around the corner on Grove Street. I'm working graveyard shift, and Reuven can spend the night.

LEARNING TO WELD

ଟ୍ଟ

August 1966. I want to learn how to weld. Ned says I need a regular job, not a temporary position at the post office. I learn that, if I work at the U.S. Naval Shipyard at Hunter's Point, I can take welding at night.

I'm lucky. The Civil Rights Act passed in 1964. I apply at the shipyard, and they hire me. I don't tell them I have a son. It's the navy. Routine, order, proper. I put down I'm single (true) on the application. I'm hired to run the tool room for the U.S.S. *Midway*, a big carrier ship.

I like the tool room. I like the feeling of the jackhammer, the tap wrenches, the center punches, the tools, the hard metal. I put the tools back in the bins, I take them out when someone comes in and asks for a plug, a drill, a ratchet.

The tool room is in an enclosed area. Outside is the open, cement-floored area where the machinists work. Men go to their stations and ream out a piece for the boat. There's a crane that the guys climb up and drive across the big concrete room. I look out of the tool room to the machinists. I look out to see the boats, the *Midway*, the *Enterprise* in dock being repaired. I look out from my little walled-in tool room and want to be out there, out there in the shipyard, out there with the sounds of overhead moving machines, the sounds of hammers pounding, the sounds of men talking, the world I know, the world I don't know, something foreign, something familiar.

When I go outside into the yard, I see the metal, stacked. I see sparks. I see men holding torches, welding, putting metal together. You're not supposed to look at the fire directly. It can hurt your eyes. I know that. But I can't help staring, watching the sparks, watching the metal heat up, fuse together.

My first day, a tall, stocky man comes in and says, "I want a female socket and a male plug and an Allen wrench. My face turns red. How am I going to handle these guys? I stand there. The only tools I know are a hammer and a screwdriver. A tall quiet man whispers to me, "There really are a female socket and a male plug."

Lunchtime—a big, big cafeteria, maybe a thousand workers getting served. Me, the only woman. Rows of men sitting there eating, rows of men getting stoned, rows of men making crude jokes. It feels familiar. Home. The guys try to include me. "Hey, Waldman, sit with us!" I hear. Mostly, I stay by myself. The smell of marijuana fills the room. I see joints being passed around. I see glazed eyes looking down on the machinery after lunch. I'm shocked. This is the United States Navy, not Haight-Ashbury, not the post office.

I start taking welding Monday nights. I put on leather chaps, leather jacket, leather gloves, and a hood with a plastic face shield. All men's sizes, too big for me. I learn about striking an arc, running the electrode across the metal plate to make a connection and then make fire. I hold the torch, put in an electrode, strike an arc by touching the electrode to the metal.

Electrodes—Carrier Clinic. 1961. They're fastening electrodes to my head, one on each side. "No!" I scream. "Let me out." Someone I can't see says, "Increase the voltage." When I wake up, I don't know where I am.

Now, it's 1966. I'm at the shipyard. I'm the one controlling the electrode. I hold the torch and strike an arc between the metal and the rod. The fire lights up the darkness. I make a pool of molten metal and join pieces together.

I forget the outside world. I forget I have a kid to support. I forget I have to pay bills. I just watch my hand move to a rhythm, watching the fire, the fusing of the metal. I don't want to go back to my house. I don't want to shop or cook or do laundry. I want to stay here and weld, put the pieces of metal together. That's what I want.

Once a week isn't enough. I ask my boss to transfer me to welding. He says I need to talk to the admiral. I've seen the admiral. A few times a month, he comes into the tool room and orders me to fetch a tool. He doesn't bother to sign out the way the workers have to. I walk into the admiral's office. He's sitting behind his huge desk in a uniform covered with pins and ribbons. He doesn't stand up or shake my hand.

"What can I do for you?"

"I would like to be transferred to the welding department. The foreman told me to talk to you."

He scratches his belly, laughs. "No. I don't want any girls welding. There was too much hanky-panky during the war."

"Please. I *have* to weld."

"You're dismissed."

Hunter's Point Riots

§

September 27, 1966. Riots. The National Guard has been called in. Shops are closing up in the Fillmore. There's a curfew. I've got to get to Reuven. At the corner of Grove, I reach Effie's and run up the stairs.

"Girl, how did you get here?" she says. "Don't you know what's happening? There's riots—here and Hunter's Point. Girl, you got to get out of here. This ain't no place for a white girl."

"I gotta take Reuven. I'll go to my house."

"Girl, you can't take care of him now. It's not safe out there. You leave him with me. He'll be okay. Come back in a day or two, after all this shit quiets down."

"I can't leave him, Effie." But I know she's right. Out the window, I see dozens of young men, shouting and running. There's not a white face anywhere. Reuven looks up, blond hair touches my face.

"I can't leave him, Effie."

"Girl, you don't got no choice. Get out now." She opens the door and waves for me to leave. I go down the stairs in a daze. People flow past me on the sidewalk. I look up. Effie holds Reuven to the window. I'll never see him again. I know it.

I see them marching this way, hundreds of them in unison. Black boots in line, gas masks, rifles—the National Guard marching down Fillmore Street. Young black men are shaking their fists and shouting.

"The pigs are coming. The pigs are coming."

I run, the only white women in a crowd of black men on Fillmore Street. I don't know where I'm going—just running away from the soldiers marching down Fillmore Street, from angry black men shouting, "Down with the pigs."

I go back to my room and stare out the window. The streets are empty now.

Early the next morning. A crack of sunlight under the door. Reuven. I've got to get to Reuven. I find my way back to Grove Street. It's eerily quiet. I see broken windows, broken glass, broken doors. Empty boxes and garbage are strewn in the street. Sheets of newspaper blow in the wind. Only a few people about. No one says anything to me. I walk up the stairs at Effie's and see my blond-haired baby sitting quietly. I go and hug him tight. I hug him some more.

Effie says, "It's quiet now. Guess you'll have to go back to work."

Work. I hadn't thought about work. I take Reuven, and we walk to my room on Steiner Street. I call the shipyard. "Report to work tomorrow," the guy says. I bring Reuven back to Effie's. Maybe tomorrow they'll start to clean up the streets.

CATY TAKES REUVEN

ೞ

January 1968.
The walls crawl.
Bugs up and down.
Black bugs.
Blue bugs.
Bugs come out of me.
I can't take it. No, Ned, I can't stand it. Take him away.
No more.
I don't want the screaming. My ears shut. Shut down now.
The crying, the diapers.
My brother, Paul. Little boy wrapped in white. Body held tight.
Make him lie still so he can't scratch.
No more.
He's gotta get away from me. I don't want it anymore. It's too much.
I slam against the wall.
I slam against my insides.
Why did I do this? Why?
Ned says, "Do you want to go ahead with adoption?"
"I want him away from me. I can't stand the crying. I can't stand it."
"Okay," says Ned. "I told you. I'll support you any way. You have a long way to go, but someday you'll be well."

"Okay, okay."

"Do you want me to call Social Services and make arrangements?" he asks.

Arrangements—I hate fuckin' arrangements. Just get him away from me.

"Well, we have to make plans," he tells me. "I'll see what I can do."

The next day Ned calls. "Okay. I've made arrangements. Beryt says she wants to take Reuven to her place for a while before the adoption. The others will help." Beryt works for Ned. Tall, smart Beryt tells Ned, "Reuven can come to my place."

Reuven's been staying with Effie ever since he was a year old. He's now two and a half. He isn't walking. He isn't talking. Effie doesn't let him play in the park and get dirty. He just stares, won't move. He's gotta get away from me, away from Effie. I don't know what's going to happen to him. I don't care anymore. I can't do it. Is there a God? Why? Why did I get into this? I can't take care of a kid. I can't take care of myself. No more. Ned, no more. Take him away. Away.

The last day I go to pay Effie. Reuven's going to be put up for adoption. I've decided. That's it. No more. I go in, hand Effie the twenty-five dollars. I don't want to step into the apartment. I stand by the door. She takes the money. I see Reuven in the background.

"Why don't you say goodbye to him, girl?" Effie's got him dressed up in a little boy outfit, shorts and a white top. He's standing by a chair, holding on. He still can't walk at two and a half. He sees me. I walk toward him. I don't want to tell him I'm leaving, leaving for good. I'm not going to give him a big hug. Just want to touch him, say goodbye. He starts to cry when he sees me. The tears come down his scrunched up face. The tears come down my stoic face.

"All right, girl," says Effie, "you better leave now." I start to run down the stairs. I've got to get off of Grove Street.

I hear pounding. I look up. Effie has Reuven at the window, the large window that opens with a crank. The window isn't open, but he is clawing at the window. I've never seen anything like it—how does he know? He knows. No one has to tell him. He knows I'm leaving. He's never going to see me again. The red face, his hands pushing, pushing against the closed window. I look up. My heart stops. What have I done?

Why, why is this happening? How can I do this to my baby? I chose to keep him, and now, look, I've ruined his life. Will I ever forget his face, his look, his hands outstretched, Mama, Mama, don't leave me?

The bugs crawl out of me and over me. I want to die.

I walk out to Fillmore Street. I walk out of his life.

Reuven stays with Beryt for about six weeks in her big sprawling apartment on the Panhandle. I don't see him, but I hear at the Foundation how Beryt, Mary, Estelle, the others are caring for him. He crawls from room to room, calling my name. He sits and stares. He won't take a bath. He screams. He screams my name, Joan, Joan, Joan.

Slowly, every day, Beryt or Estelle or Mary play with him by the bathtub. A splash. Very slowly, he lets them touch him; very slowly, he lets them take off his clothes. Taking off his shirt and putting the washrag to his chest. Scream. Scream. And then in a week or two, no scream, and then off come his pants. Just like that. Piece by piece. Moment by moment.

Ned tells me plans for the adoption are going through. Social Services is working on it. He'll have a good family.

Family. What's that? My skin crawls. *Me holding Paul, open sores, scratch, scratch, wrapped in muslin, don't move.*

The day comes. Reuven's to be moved to foster care. The day comes for me to sign papers. The social worker comes to Ned's office. I start running back and forth in the narrow hall. A social worker dressed in a navy knit suit. I used to dress in a navy knit suit. A social worker says sign here.

I get up. "No, no, no. Ned, I can't. I just can't. I don't want him going anyplace else."

"What are you going to do, Joan?"

"I don't know."

"Well, let's think about it. Maybe he can go back to Effie's for a while, but if he does, you can't scream at her anymore. Call me when you want to scream. Okay?"

"Okay, I'll call."

"I'll talk to Effie and see if she'll take him back. I'll see her so we know what's happening. Is that all right with you?"

I don't know. The bugs crawl back into the walls, at least for now. I stop scratching, at least for now.

Reuven stays with Effie until Caty says, "He's gotta get out of there. He's not walking; he's not talking." I call my parents for money to pay Caty. No, they won't give me money, but they tell me I have a bond in my name. I can cash that. Fine. So Caty says, "Okay," as she needs money, and she genuinely cares about Reuven.

He moves around the corner to Steiner Street—the Victorian house on Steiner across from Alamo Park, an old floor-through, a big apartment with the lights from the park shining in. Caty's kids are close to Reuven's age. He can have a brother and a sister. He can have a family. I'm glad. I can have a family.

Now Caty has three kids in diapers, three kids with no help from Steve. No money for a car. No help from me. But Caty's used to handling chaos.

One day I'm sitting in my room down the block, my big room in the artist's co-op. The phone rings. It's Caty. "Come over right away," she says. "You won't believe it." I grab my backpack and leave. When I get to Caty's, Reuven is running up and down the long flight of stairs, up and down the steep stairs, up and down the many stairs. "Look!" Caty screams, "Look, he won't stop." The little boy who wouldn't stand up, the little boy who wouldn't walk—he's now running up the stairs. John is saying, "Yea, Roov." He calls him Roov. Caty is screaming, "Yea, Roov." I don't know what to do, but I'm glad.

The same thing happens with talking. He won't talk, and then one day, I'm visiting, and he starts with full sentences. I'm there almost daily. The kids, running around the apartment, riding trikes, screaming, wearing no diapers, often having rashes on their bottoms. We're into freedom—kids should be free. No diapers—that's groovy.

Sometimes I take Reuven home for the night to my room in the artists' co-op. I have a double mattress on the floor, and we both sleep on it. One night he won't go to sleep. I read him a story and another, but he won't go to sleep. Finally, we're both knocked out. When it's black outside in the hardcore night, he wakes up screaming, shaking. I'm still asleep. I yell, "Shhh, the baby's sleeping."

Next to me on the mattress, he says in a small voice, "What baby?"

I look around. Where did my words come from? My mother. My brother and me. I get scared. I'm becoming my mother. Oh no! I stroke his forehead and say, "I know there's no baby."

THE ONLY WAY OUT IS THROUGH

❧

March 1968. It's past midnight. I'm working for the post office again. I've just finished another evening sorting mail in between tokes. I walk up the stairs, step by step, to the front room with bay windows in Caty's house on Steiner Street. Tears are coming down my cheek. I don't know where I am. I shiver. I want something familiar—Caty, someone to be with me. I don't plan to stay long—just want to check in. I trip over the toy truck. The three kids are still up. Reuven tugs at my leg. I keep walking. Caty puts the kids to bed on the mattress on the floor in the front room, the mattress that we found outside on the sidewalk. I don't kiss Reuven good night. I don't want to see him.

I go to the side room and look out the bay window. We're on the top floor, and I can see the lights of the city swirling around me. The light hits my eyes. I'm floating off in the sky. That's where I want to live, in the sky.

Caty comes into the room where I'm standing. The room is empty except for a chair and the mattress from the street and a table from Goodwill that cost five dollars. We like finding used or thrown-out furniture. To me, it's finding a new way, a way out of the world of Hillside, New Jersey, away from the diamond rings, suburban homes my high school friends are either aspiring to or already living in.

Caty sees me, but she's talking to the air. Pacing back and forth across the room. I hear her slam down a pot she's holding. "I don't know what's going to happen. We can't live here anymore. Steve lost that job he got. I don't have any money. I need to see Ned."

Caty. She's tall, thin, and stately. Since I've known Caty, five or six years, she wears one pair of shoes—Zorrie flip-flops. She wears them inside the house and outside, to go shopping, to go to the Foundation, to go to the park, anywhere, and Caty is wearing her Zorrie flip-flops now, her Zorrie flip-flops and a plain small floral housedress with a tie in the back.

I know I should be grateful she is taking care of Reuven, but I don't want to hear about it tonight. I don't want to be in this house on Steiner Street. I don't want to be in my one room on Steiner Street down the block. I don't want to *be* anymore.

I look out at the park. I don't know what's different about tonight, but I want to dive into the dirt. The lights from the park have gone out. I put my head down. The kids are finally asleep. Steve isn't home. We don't know where he is. He could be at the Foundation, he could be down the street, shooting the breeze with Dau, Turtle, and the others who hang out on Haight Street.

There's a bed. A single mattress put up against the windowsill. I lie down. "Caty, I'm going to stay the night."

I get up and throw some cold water on my face. My nightgown's in the closet. I sometimes stay overnight. I don't want to be alone. I want to have a family. Even Caty's mixed-up family is okay.

I stare out the window into the darkness. My breath is shallow. My heart is pounding. I keep looking out. I open the window and stick my head out. I can feel the fresh air on me. My head is out the window, out the ledge. The dark is calling to me. The rest of me is inside on tiptoe. I'm holding on, gripping my fingers around the window's edge.

Caty hears the window go up and comes in. It's very late—early morning. "Yikes," she shrieks. She grabs my nightgown and pulls on me. "What are you doing?"

"No, leave me alone."

I see the lights in my mind. I want to fly to them outside.

"Leave me alone."

She closes the window.

"I'm going to call Ned."

She calls his office and hands me the phone. It rings and rings and then, to my amazement, a voice, a sleepy voice answers. Caty takes the phone from me and says, "Ned, she has her head out the window. What should I do?"

"Put her on."

"Ned, I can't go on like this. I can't stand it. I don't want to live anymore. Please leave me alone."

"*Nu*, you've hung on so long. It's already three in the morning. A few more hours won't make that much difference. Come see me in the morning. Be here at eight o'clock. You can do it."

I hear the Jewish word *nu*, and I smile. "Okay, okay."

I put on my long skirt from the thrift store, my long earrings, my short sleeveless top, and I sit on the bed, staring out into the empty room, rubbing my hands against my skirt and wait and wait until seven fifteen when it is time to take the #22 Fillmore bus up to Ned's office.

I walk up the long flight of stairs I've walked up so many times to see Ned. He greets me at the door. He is wearing the same white shirt he always wears—the same short sleeves with the collar turned up, and fine pieces of blond-gray hairs on his chest showing. His plain black belt holds up his pants over his thick belly. He smiles.

"Come into my office."

"Why do I have to keep doing this? I'm here almost every day, and I can't stand it. I can't stand it. All I do is go to work, come here, and see Reuven. My head spins."

Ned's body walks toward me. I scream.

"Get out. Leave me alone."

"Joan, where are you?"

"I don't know."

"Where are you?"

Someone big is coming at me. I duck.

"Stay with it," he says.

I run from one end of the room to the other.

He keeps walking to me, one step at a time.

I duck. He throws me against the wall.

I cover my head.

I know he's going to kill me.

Ned stoops down beside me.

He whispers, "Joan, where are you? Where are you?"

"Get away," I scream. "I want to go home."

I jump up and manage to get the door open. Ned moves swiftly and closes it again.

"Joan, where are you?"

I fall to the floor again. "I don't know," I sob. "I just want to go home."

"No, stay."

He leaves.

I pound at the door.

"Let me out, let me out." *He's trying to kill me.* "Let me out. I'm going to call the police."

Ned walks back. Minutes later, maybe an hour. He closes the door. He walks toward me to grab my hand.

I scream, "You're going to kill me. I know it."

Time passes. The morning, the afternoon. I'm drenched in sweat. All day.

I'm in the basement of my father's store. My friend Ernie isn't here. I don't want to be doing this, mister! I don't want to be doing this, mister! Let's go and get my daddy!

Ned keeps saying, "Stay with it."

"I just want to go home."

"Stay with it."

"It's dark in here. I can't stand it. Let me out."

Ned leaves for a while.

I pound on the door.

He comes back toward me.

He's going to kill me. He's mad.

Hey, Joe, look what we have here! Come here, little girl. Hold her down! Don't let her go, goddam it!"

"But she's such a little thing."

"She's the boss's daughter, ain't she? Goddam cunt! That's what they all are! Hold her legs. I'm going in. Now, you be a good girl, and you listen to Mr. Lester. Mr. Lester is a good man. Mr. Lester cares about you. Mr.

Lester cares about little white girls. Now, you just pick up your dress, and you let Mr. Lester see what's under that dress. Go ahead. You do that for Mr. Lester, or Mr. Lester is going to get very mad. Now, you let Joe pull down your panties. We want to see what you have under those pretty panties. That's a good girl. Goddam it, Joe! I'm going in first."

I scream, "Daddy, no, I'll be good! Please, Daddy, I'll be good."

It's dark inside now, very dark.

Back and forth.

Inside and out.

I don't know where I am, in the dark, with my daddy coming at me down the steps where it's dark. My panties are down. Blood is coming down my legs. I've fainted. My father's screaming, "Look at you. Get upstairs."

He's mad, my daddy. He's going to kill me. I'm going to die. Oh, my bottom hurts, I can't walk. "Daddy, it hurts."

"Get upstairs if you know what's good for you, young lady. Get upstairs. And you—get back to work. Get those boxes moving."

I see light. Ned touches my shoulder. "It's all over, Joan. It's over. No one is going to hurt you. Go home. Get some sleep. Come back tomorrow morning at ten o'clock. Good work."

I walk out of the building, and the sun has gone down.

Waiting for the #22 bus, I remember the dark basement. I remember when I had shock treatments and I could feel the basement, the hand pulling my underpants down, and I thought the therapist would hear me, but he didn't. He gave me Thorazine.

Ned's words come into my ears, "If we face the pain, we will survive. We'll come through. You'll come through."

NED DIES

&

May 1968. Harry calls a special session. The Foundation, all of us, crowd into the front room on Fillmore Street. Plain chairs, sitting, waiting. Where's Harry? Ned is away on a trip. Sounds in the room, sounds reverberate. Talk. I wait. I sit. What does Harry want? Why did he call this special meeting?

Tall, thin Harry. His dark hair falls over his face. He bursts into the front room, the old Victorian room. Everyone is seated.

He takes a few steps into the room and says in a flat voice, "Ned died. In the airport in Salt Lake City. Heart attack."

That's it. Harry disappears the way he in came in, fast. What? What? I hear cries, sobs, people standing, screaming, standing, sitting. How can it be? He's dead. How? What? The room is chaotic, like on a tight subway with the clacking of the train that drowns out the noise of all kinds.

Oh, my God!

What's going to happen?

What's going to happen to me?

Then I get up. I've got to get away from the click, clacking all around me. I slowly walk down the stairs from Ned's office onto Fillmore Street. Then I turn around and slowly walk back up the stairs, steep stairs. I walk to the top. I don't hear the cries now, the sobs. At the top I see Ned.

He is looking at me. His open shirt, his big belly, his wide smile. He's looking at me, and he goes to grab my hands, and I am looking at Ned. Looking at Ned for the first time, although I've seen him hundreds of times through the few years I've been coming to his office.

I look and something in my head says, "I don't know you, Ned. I don't know who you are. I've only been seeing what I can see—you said that to me my first session—I'm seeing through rose-colored glasses. I'm not seeing as it is. And I realize I've never seen you." And my feet start to move, and I start to move. I look, and I'm dancing, I'm free. I can feel it. For the first time in my life, I'm free. So strange. Ned is dead. No one for me to call and say, "I need a session." No one to yell to, "I can't take it anymore. Reuven's got to go." No one to go over to Caty or Effie or whomever else and say, "She can't handle it yet—please keep Reuven a little longer." No one to smile at me. No one to care.

So strange. My feet want to dance. My heart wants to sing. I'm alive. I run back down the long flights of the stairs. I run down, I run up. I look at the big room of sobbing people, screaming people. I know I need to grow up. I know I have to take care of myself and Reuven. I know. I just know I will be all right. I have to.

People hug. I hug, but I don't feel like hugging. I need to get out of here. I take the #22 bus down Fillmore Street. The bus I've taken so many times.

People are quick to organize. Come for a session. Come for a group.

Ned is gone.

Change.

PART 4
&
MOVING ON

DRIVING

𝄢

July 1968. I need to drive. I can't go on like this—busing to childcare, busing to the Foundation, busing to work, busing back home. I need to drive. I'm going back to school. I need to drive over the Bay Bridge to Laney College for welding classes.

But it's been so many years since I've driven. The ghosts. I've lived with the ghosts—the basement, the dark. How can I steer straight ahead, know when to turn, know how to watch out for an oncoming car?

I look for someone who can help. Hector! Hector from the Foundation. Hector rebuilds cars. Hector, with his strong Argentinean accent, his bright red hair. Hector understands my situation. About a week later, he says, "I have a little Renault I just rebuilt. It's a perfect car for you—small. I'll even give you a good price."

"A Renault? I don't need any foreign car."

"Give it a try. You have nothing to lose."

"But Hector, I haven't driven in over ten years. I wouldn't know what to do."

"Give it a try. I'll go out with you."

He comes over to my apartment in the Haight with the Renault. I've never driven a stick shift. He shows me. I lurch forward. I lurch backward. I don't have a license. Step by step, we go through the process.

Step by step, Hector shows me how to drive, takes me to get my license. I pass. I can drive the Renault.

But the Renault doesn't drive. I call Hector. He comes and fixes it. It still doesn't drive well. It never does. There's usually something wrong with it. Finally, he takes it back and trades it for an American car that works.

I start driving. I find out that I've changed. I can do things I couldn't do a few years ago. Foundation people notice. I'm coming into the world.

WELDING SCHOOL

ℬ

September 1968. My first day of welding school. Laney College, Oakland, California. I walk into a large room, dark, low overhead lights, benches and metal tables around the outside, dirt floor on the inside, piles of metal—little piles, big piles on the side. Machines, arc welders, acetylene torches, cutting saws, chipping hammers, brushes. Each worktable has a few pieces of metal on it. Smells of burning, smells of fire, smells of the shipyard.

I walk into silence. The room has stopped buzzing. Eyes are on me. Mr. Colville is standing in front of me. He's a big man in jeans and a leather jacket with a big belt holding some tools. "Get your leathers and helmet and get to your place. I heard you were coming. Don't know why you would want to do this nasty work, but keep out of trouble, and you'll be okay."

The first day. "Okay, we're here to weld. Anyone not in the right class, leave now. We're going to learn to weld, and we're going to learn about metal—its malleability, its other properties, and we're going to learn about safety. We don't want any accidents—hear that all of you? You're gonna learn to be careful around fire—fire can make or break you."

He looks at Pete and says, "Okay, now. Get your sweetheart set up and make sure she doesn't burn the place down."

I'm used to this talk. I've heard it before—at the shipyard, only there I had the admiral and three thousand men. Now, I'm in a class of fifteen, and my good friend Pete is in his second year. He told me about Laney College. Short, wiry Pete, with a Budweiser in his hand. He keeps an eye out for me. I know how to strike an arc from my class at the shipyard, but I don't know much else. I'm determined to learn.

Every day I come to class. Every day I drive over the Bay Bridge, leave Reuven off at daycare, go to class, drive back to the daycare, pick him up, and drive across town to our apartment in Noe Valley—a lot of driving to follow my passion. All I know is I've got to learn to weld, to strike the arc, see the fire.

That first day, I go outside during break. I see stares. I'm the only woman with leathers on, the only woman learning a trade. In the cafeteria, an older woman comes up to me. She's wearing an apron and a chef's hat—she works in the cafeteria. She says, "Oh, I haven't seen this in years—not since the war. You know, I was a riveter in the war." She tells me all her friends worked for the war effort, but now no one works, or they're working in the cafeteria like her. "No jobs like there used to be." She says, "Good luck, honey!" and she goes back behind the counter.

ℬ

May 1969. I come out of class during break. Noise all around. People talking. Tension everywhere.

"What's going on?" I ask.

A guy with a long beard and sandals says, "Haven't you heard, lady? People's Park got fired on." He points north. "The cops are shooting people. Those goddam pigs! Oh God, we gotta get some guns and shoot the hell out of them."

I freeze. Another riot. When will it end?

ℬ

Summertime. I bring hash brownies to class, hash brownies I've made. Mr. Colville sees me give brownies to Pete and to Mike and some of the other guys. I don't offer them to Mr. Colville, but he keeps staring at them, so I finally say, "Mr. Colville, would you like a brownie?"

"You make 'em?" he asks.

"Sure."

"Okay, I'll take one," and he eats it. I don't say anything. I give him one and another and another. He says they taste swell. I look at Pete and Mike. Our tall teacher in overalls starts slurring his words. His eyes are lit up. Our tall teacher is stoned. I decide not to bring hash brownies to class again.

I learn real slowly, preparing the metal, making welds flat, vertical, overhead. Over and over, we practice—make practice plates. Then I learn to test the plates to see if they hold. The smell, the darkness, the light. I'm home. I know it. I don't know why, but I know I'm home.

MEETING TURK

❦

June 1969. I'm hanging out at the Boneyard where Pete lives at the edge of Berkeley, not in the hills, but the edge leading to the freeway. The Boneyard—hippies and druggies live at the Boneyard. It's a big lot with old trucks, old school buses, old equipment, rusted and worn. A place where the end-of-the-road hippies hang out, where dope passes from one to another, where bodies crash for the night.

I visit Pete. Holding a beer in one hand, he walks me around, showing me his welding equipment. "This here is my friend, Turk," he says when we pass a worn, parked school bus. Big-belly Turk, curly-haired Turk. He got the name Turk because he was born in Turkey. Turk shows us around his home, the school bus. It leaks. There are puddles on the floor. It doesn't move. It's got a curtain over the window where he has a platform bed. A little kitchen. A little rusty, but you can heat water. No fridge.

I start visiting the Boneyard with Reuven, start visiting Turk in his broken-down school bus. He's taking a trip. Getting out of Berkeley. Where? "Man, I don't know. Just out of here." Do I want to come? Bring Reuven too?

"Sure," I say.

"Just gotta fix the bus a little, and we can go." It happens. We leave Berkeley, slowly crawling away in the old bus. The first night it rains. It pours. Rain comes through the windows, rain comes through the roof.

"Damn," Turk says. "I thought it was all sealed up." We stop.

He tells me his story. It touches me. Deeply. He was raised in a boarding school in DC. His father—a diplomat from Turkey. His mother—a prostitute? Not clear. He spends his childhood alone in a boarding school. The other kids go home for the holidays. His father doesn't come. He stays at the school with a matron.

The bond between us is forged. We sleep together. His warm body engulfs me—keeps me safe. I tell him I don't have a boyfriend. "Why?" he asks. Shrug my shoulders. No one likes me. He holds me. At the Boneyard, I'm sort of Turk's "old lady." I'm nine years older than he is, with a five-year-old son.

Reuven and I move into a cute cottage in back of a house on Valencia Street for fifty dollars a month. Turk kind of moves in, kind of visits, kind of leaves. Is there, isn't there. Wants to help with Reuven. Doesn't have any money. Needs a place to sleep.

I have a boyfriend. Two lonely people. He listens. He understands. The nights of being with a man, having a boyfriend. He'll walk me through, he says.

I'm twenty-nine. I should have a boyfriend. Turk says he'll stay with me. Maybe, I'll be okay. Maybe, I won't be such a freak. I want a boyfriend like the other girls. I want. Will he really be my boyfriend? No one has ever wanted me. I like talking to him. What does that mean? I don't know.

Up North

 ☙

T urk has been working on that old motorcycle he got from the junkyard.

"Can't stay here forever and let the draft catch up with me," he says one day. "Taking a road trip. I want to see the world. Don't wait for me. I'll be gone at least a year."

He kick-starts the Harley and flies down Valencia, a green army backpack strapped to the back of his bike.

A few days later, the phone rings. It's Turk.

"The fucking Harley threw a rod. Can you come get me?"

"Where are you?"

"Mendocino."

I drive the VW bus I bought recently up to Mendocino. Turk gives me a quick kiss. His hands and clothes are black with grease. He straps the Harley to the back of the bus with a thick chain.

He takes the wheel, doesn't say much.

For an hour, I watch the scenery. The redwoods, the mountains, the road twisting.

"So, what are you going to do?" I finally say.

"Fix it. What do you think?" he says.

After a while, he softens. "Shouldn't take much."

"Cool."

Silence.

Then Turk says, "I'm thinking of heading north, maybe up to Washington State."

He glances over at me, then looks back to the road.

"Why don't you come with me?"

I don't say anything, but every muscle in my body tenses. Does he really want to make a life with me?

"Pete's up in Bellingham, welding in a shipyard. Maybe he can help you score a job. You ain't got nothing going around here, anyway."

Ned's gone; the shipyard in California won't hire a woman. "All right, I'll think about it."

The next day, Reuven comes home crying.

"What happened?"

"Some kids hit me with a water bomb, and one of the big kids tripped me and yelled, 'White boy go home.'"

"Do you know the kids?"

"Yeah, they live down the street."

We live in the Mission District in a three-room cottage with peeling white paint. We're the only white family in the neighborhood. We're the only ones who don't go to church. This scene isn't working for us. I don't know what I want, but something starts moving inside me. I start clearing out trash, stuff that we don't need.

One day I come back to the house after taking a load of old papers to the garbage area. Reuven is standing at the door with his little backpack, ready to go. He folds his arms and says, "If you're going, I'm going too."

That does it. I tell Turk we're going.

Three days later, we're on our way to Bellingham—Turk, Reuven, and I. At first, we crash on the floor at Pete's house. Then one day when I'm driving around near the college, I see a big white house with a sign on the lawn. For Rent: 3 bedrooms, $75 a month. I find a phone and call the number.

"I need first and last month's rent," the man says.

I tell him I'm a single mother with a five-year-old.

"OK, lady, whatever. A hundred fifty bucks and you can move in."

Back at Pete's, a handful of guys and a few women are hanging out, smoking joints, mumbling. There's nothing to eat. One hundred and fifty dollars. Turk doesn't have it. I sure don't. But I really want that house.

I haven't spoken to my parents in years. Pete lets me use the phone. I call collect.

Someone picks up on the third ring. "Hello?"

"Hi, Ma."

"Oh, it's you. Here, talk to your father."

"Joan? Is that you? What's going on? Where are you?"

"I'm in Bellingham, Washington. Up near Canada."

"Bellingham? Never heard of it. What's going on there? What's all that racket?"

"Just some people. I'm at somebody's house. Dad, I need to borrow some money ..."

"No, you can't borrow money. You need to come home, Joan. What are you doing in Canada, or wherever the hell it is?"

"I can't come home. I have Reuven. I've found a nice place for us to live. I just need—"

"Where are you? I can't hear a thing you're saying."

"Washington State. I just need to borrow some money. Just for a little while. So we can get a place to live."

"Who are you living with, and what's all that noise?"

"It's just the stereo. Someone turned it up too loud."

"I don't like you being there." He pauses. "Are you connected to that Manson Gang I've heard about?"

"For God's sake, Dad, no. These are just some friends of mine. I don't know anyone in the Manson Gang."

"Are you sure? What a racket. Can't you get a job? A little hard work never stopped me. Get yourself a job. Here, talk to your mother."

"Why don't you get a job? Doesn't anybody out there work?"

"I can't get a job right now, Mom. I need a place to live first. I have Reuven."

"You can work in a store, as your father did. They're always looking for cashiers. Here, talk to your father."

"What kind of people are you hanging around with out there? Do any of them even have jobs? Are you sure they're not part of that Manson Gang?"

"Dad, just this once. I won't bother you for money again."

"I wouldn't send you a red cent if I thought you were hanging around with criminals."

"I'm not, I swear."

"Don't swear. I'm not sending money if there're people there who are just going to take it away from you."

"They won't. Please …"

"How much?"

"A hundred fifty dollars."

"A hundred fifty? What do you need that much for?"

"To move into a house. First and last month's rent. For Reuven."

"All right. I'll wire it tomorrow."

We say good-bye and hang up. My hands are shaking. My legs are weak. Now I remember why I don't call my parents.

I move into the house. It's a big house that needs a lot of work, but this is the first time I've had a house of my own, a real house, and Reuven is living with me full-time. Turk has moved in too. I have a house and a family. A home.

I don't know how to keep house—how to dust or clean up. I don't know what to buy or how to cook, so every morning we have corn flakes and milk.

"I'm sick of this," Turk says.

He drives off in his truck and comes back with some eggs.

"Watch," he says to Reuven and me.

"This is how you make eggs. Hold it like this, crack it on the edge of the pan, ease it in the pan. Don't forget the margarine."

We watch as the egg cooks from clear to white.

Then he grabs the pan by the handle and flips it so the egg turns over.

"OK, give it a try."

I crack the egg, but it splatters when I try to flip it.

"Here, use the spatula. It's easier."

Now we have eggs for breakfast some days.

Turk comes and goes. He's out a lot. Sometimes, he's gone all day. He hangs out with friends I've never met, but he comes home most nights. I never know when he's coming back.

One late night, I hear his truck pull up and park. He staggers in, stinking of whiskey and pot, his eyes sleepy red orbs. I'm mad. This isn't the way boyfriends are supposed to be.

"Where were you all day?" I demand.

He weaves across the room and drops onto the old green sofa we picked up off the street.

"Out getting really wasted," he says, chuckling. "And I mean good and solid fucked-up stoned."

Then he lifts his head and glares at me. "Not that it's any of your goddam business anyways."

A few days later, I jump in my VW bus and follow him when he leaves. He drives down the hill on the Southside to a brown house with a rickety white picket fence and lots of hippies milling around outside on the porch—girls with long hair and long skirts, bearded men with ponytails and earrings. I sit in the bus across the street and watch as a joint gets passed from one person to another, everyone smoking, everyone laughing and just hanging out, having a good time. I never have times like that.

Finally I work up some guts and walk up to the porch. "Is Turk here?" I ask.

People stop talking for a moment and look at me, curious, like I'm strange or something. They look at each other and try to hide their smirks.

"Yeah, cool," a guy says. "Sit tight." He leans into the open doorway and hollers, "Hey, Turk, some old lady is looking for you."

When Turk sees me, he comes storming down the stairs. "What the hell are you doing here? I told you not to bother me."

"I want to know what you're up to."

"What I'm up to? I'm hanging out with my goddam friends, so you can beat it. Scram. Leave me the hell alone."

Turk turns his back to me and storms away. He doesn't look back. I go back to the VW and drive home, crying the whole way.

FREE SCHOOL

&

A white flier stapled to a telephone pole catches my eye.

If you want to change the world, start by changing the way we educate our children. Join us for discussions about starting our own community Free School in Bellingham. Pizza provided!

Toad Hall, Saturday, September 26, 3 p.m.

Toad Hall. A big, open room with pillars in the basement of a building on Southside. John, the owner, a slim, short-haired man with hippie ideals, is busy serving pizza to everyone while people talk among themselves or stand up and address the gathering. There are lots of parents, lots of kids.

A bearded man with long black hair and a beat-up cowboy hat stands up, shakes his fist, and shouts, "We've got to give our kids a real education! They need to learn about the world—about what's really going on out there, all the groovy stuff and all the bullshit too. These kids are bright and beautiful. We don't want their minds being corrupted by the system."

"Right on, man, right on," someone calls out.

"Free minds."

"Free spirits. Free expression," a woman's voice shouts.

"Free pizza!" a voice in the back calls out. Laughter. The woman resumes. "Let's create a school built on freedom—freedom to think what you want, freedom to learn what you want, freedom to love whom you want to love, freedom to be as beautiful as you want to be."

Agreement all around. Kids learn what interests them, at their own pace. Someone starts passing around sign-up sheets. I write my name, Reuven's name, and our address. Another meeting is planned to work out all the details. We're starting a Free School.

I see Reuven across the room and go to fetch him. He's made a new friend, a little blond kid named Scott. There's a dark-haired girl too, Scott's sister, Michelle, a year older.

"Are you Reuven's mom?" a young woman asks me. She's even shorter than I am, and she smiles a lot. "I'm Camilla."

We walk out of Toad Hall together, and she says, "Let's go grab a beer." Fairhaven Tavern is right around the corner. We let the kids run around outside and be "free."

Camilla is from Michigan. She and her husband moved their family out here to start a new life, find a new way to live. He just went back to get more of their belongings. I tell her I just moved up from San Francisco. "Cool," she says. "We'll help each other out."

I've made a friend. A friend with kids Reuven's age.

"Come on over," Camilla says, so Reuven and I drive out to the small farmhouse on Northwest Road. The house has only four rooms for the four of them—Camilla, Kent, and the two kids—plus two friends from Michigan who've been crashing there for a while.

After that day, we go there a lot. Reuven usually takes off with Scott and Michelle. They go outside and run around in the field next door, chasing the cows or finding things to play with. The outhouse is back there too. I don't like having to go out and use it with all those cows watching me.

Camilla always has a big pot of brown rice on the stove. This evening, she's standing by the old porcelain sink, chopping onions and carrots. The smell of onion is so strong, my eyes water.

"You're having dinner with us, I hope," she says in her clear, confident voice. "I've got some tofu to use up, too."

"Right on," Kent says. He's rolling a joint, spreading leafy green pot along the fold in a yellow Zig-Zag paper. "Plenty of good food here. Plenty of good smoke." He licks the paper and rolls the joint tight. "And plenty of good-looking ladies, too, for that matter."

"Love to," I say, and I mean it. The kids don't like the macrobiotic food much, but to us adults it's the only way to go. That's not the big thing, though. The real reason I want to stay here is that Camilla is my best friend. She cares about me. Reuven runs around outside with his friends, and I tell Camilla about Turk, who's become a stranger. I never know where he is or what he's doing. All I know is he comes home sometimes and has sex with me or just sleeps, then he's gone again. Here, on Northwest Road with Camilla and Kent, I see what a real home and a real family are like. It's something I thought I was going to have with Turk, but that's not the way it's working out.

By dinnertime, it's dark and cold outside. We wash the bowls and chopsticks and wipe down the big wooden table with its fifty years of cuts and scratches. Kent sets up the Monopoly game. Everyone plays—the adults, the kids, and Kent's friends. When we hear a creak from the back room in the old house or the wind outside whistles and moans through the dry corn stalks, someone whispers, "Shhh, that's the ghost of the old man who lived alone here for forty years. He died just before we moved in."

ॐ

The Free School is up and running. We found a Pentecostal Christian Church willing to rent out space in its basement and a woman named Janice to be the teacher. Some of the richer parents are going to pay her a salary.

I pick up Reuven after his first day of school.

"Well, how was it?"

"Fun."

"What did you do?"

"We went to the park and played."

"All day?"

"Almost. And we did this." He shows me a picture of a big cat he drew and colored with crayons.

Next day the kids play in the park most of the day and draw another picture. Same thing the following day.

Kent, who used to be a teacher in Michigan, decides to go and help out.

I ask him how it's going.

"Far fucking out," he says. "Totally copacetic. The kids are free, man, like totally free."

They're free, but I wonder, is Reuven learning?

Welding Shop

§

Spring 1971. When Camilla and Kent buy a red log cabin in Wickersham, Reuven and I take over the "ghost" house on Northwest Road. Fifty dollars a month for a small farmhouse. Two small bedrooms with a garage and a barn and a large field spread out past the narrow roadway leading up from the road. I want to grow vegetables. I want to be self-sustaining and heat the house with the wood stove.

Biggy, the local fix-it man. drives up in his beat-up 1950 Ford. He looks over at the garage. He looks straight at me. "Hey, lady welder, why don't you put a welding shop in here?" I wonder, "Can I do it?" Will customers come by, say, "Hey lady, would you fix this for me?" Or bring a truck into the driveway and ask me to weld a broken piece of metal?

Biggy leaves me standing in the driveway. Me, wanting a welding shop, me wanting to make money welding for the locals, for the farmers, for those who want simple jobs. After all, I learned welding from a master. He was always kind to me, and I learned how to punch, how to work with the metal, how to put two pieces together. And here on Northwest Road, along with the small house and the big barn, there's the tin garage with the dirt floor. That could be my shop.

I get equipment for the shop. I look around. I go to an auction. I go around town, asking for equipment. I get most of it used, most of it from auctions and yard sales. A small Lincoln arc welder, a table saw, a table with a vise, a hammer. And a torch. An oxyacetylene torch that I light with a spark lighter. I borrow a truck to haul the equipment.

I have an image: me, the single mom; me, the lady welder; me, having my own shop. But I didn't grow up fixing things around the house. Women didn't fix things then. I can do the welding, but preparing the metal, working with it … I don't know how. I'll ask, I'll learn.

Biggy does help me set up the shop. "Here, woman," he says, "let me show you how to prepare the metal so you can weld it." He picks up a wire brush and scrapes the steel. Then he leaves.

Now, I'm alone. I look at the little shop. It's here under a tin roof with a dirt floor. Who am I to have a welding shop? But this is what I want. I want to touch the welder, the vise. I want to smell the metal, see the torch near me, see the flame as I strike an arc. I don't know why, but I want to put my hood on, to feel the darkness and then the light coming up.

CLYDE

ℬ

Winter 1971. I didn't realize I would be alone—alone in a farmhouse with a six-year-old. Alone, I have to chop wood, keep a fire going, get food, cook food, get Reuven dressed and out of the house to the Free School. I can't do it. I can't cook. I can't chop wood. Reuven eats cereal most of the time and defrosted frozen chicken from the package that he's learned to heat up himself.

Reuven comes in.

"There's no kindling," he sighs. "Here, this is what's left," and he puts the two logs down by the fire.

"Okay, I'll buy some."

The wind is howling. The house is cold. I drive into town and go see Biggy. He fixes cars and trucks, and he knows where to get things.

"Biggy, I need some wood. We're freezing. Where can I buy some?"

"I'll get you a couple of cords. I'll drive it out in the afternoon."
He does.

The ground is too hard to plant now. I need to wait until spring. I go to the co-op I helped start. Bag some grains, bag some veggies. Every day back and forth, light the fire, keep it going.

"Hey, Joan." I hear a voice in the co-op. "Hey, I hear you're living out on Northwest Road. I hear there's a big field out there."

Reuven is by my side.

"Hey, Reuv," the voice says, " how would you like to have a horse to ride? He's old, but he would be perfect for you—he would go slow so you can learn."

"I don't know how to ride."

"No problem. I'll show you how, and I'll throw in the saddle. We can't keep Clyde anymore. Clyde would be great for you."

Reuven looks at me. His eyes are pleading.

"I don't know how to care for a horse."

"Please," Reuven says. "I'll take care of him."

"Sure," the voice says, "I'll show him."

"All right," I say slowly.

"I'll bring him over this weekend. I'll bring everything you need."

"Okay."

Clyde arrives in a trailer, not the fancy horse trailers we see going out to the county fair but a beat-up trailer. Reuven runs out to see Clyde. There he is. Yup, he's old, he's a nag. but he has a soft coat, a brushed mane, and alert eyes. My friend walks Clyde to the field. Reuven follows. I lag behind. I don't like animals, especially big animals like horses, but Reuven wants him. Maybe it'll be fun. I'll learn to ride. Reuven will learn to ride. My friend shows us how to feed Clyde.

"Here take a scoop of feed and put it in the bucket," he says. He writes a list of what I need to buy.

"All right," he says. "Good luck."

"Thanks," Reuven says as he waves goodbye.

"Thanks," I mutter.

"Come on, let's go in."

"No, I want to stay out here with Clyde. Can't I sleep with him tonight?"

"Reuven, you can't sleep in the field all night. Now, get in the house. You can come out and feed him in the morning before school."

When I wake up, I look out the window and see Reuven going out to the field, climbing over the fence. He goes into the barn and gets the bucket and holds it out for Clyde. I see Reuven jump back. Clyde comes toward him wanting more food. Reuven, his small frame against Clyde's big body, jumps backwards, crawls under the fence and runs back to the house.

"Clyde doesn't want his food," he says.

I go out there. Clyde is galloping around with his legs up high. What is he doing? What should I do? I run into the barn, get the bucket of food, put it beside him, jump over the fence, and run back to the house.

This becomes our pattern. Reuven doesn't want to go out there. I don't want to go out there, but I do. Twice a day I go out, leave the food in the bucket. I do like looking at Clyde—a lone figure in the field. I like the open field. But I don't do the things needed to care for an animal. I don't pet him, I don't brush him. I just don't. Clyde stays in the open field by himself, slowly walking back and forth.

I don't mind going out to leave food for Clyde in the fall. But then winter comes. The rains come. The wind comes. I step into puddles of mud as the wind is howling. I can't do this anymore. I just can't. No more, and I stop going out there. Clyde whines and whines. It's a chore to keep the fire going—the wind blows, and the fire wants to blow out. It's a chore starting the van. It's hard being on Northwest Road alone with Reuven, a six-year-old.

Clyde, all alone out there, alone in the muddy field with the wind and the rain. One day he falls. I go out in the blowing winds. I don't know what to do. He struggles to get up. His front legs give out. He rests, then tries again. This time, he raises his thin body back up to stand on his feet and slowly walks back to the barn.

One day I look out, and Clyde has fallen again. He stumbles and falls, and this time he can't get up. The winds keep howling. The rain is relentless. I go out. I put my head under the fence. I fall. Tears come down. I can't do this. I don't want to do this. I scream to Reuven to go feed Clyde. He starts out, but the wind blows him down.

The next day, I don't go out. How did I get into this? What's going to happen? I look out again, and Clyde is lying on the ground. I see him start to get up. He falls again.

Barely breathing, barely able to stand up, barely able to see, Clyde is dying. Inside, I am dying. A neighbor comes by and sees Clyde and says, "I can take him away if you want." I nod. He comes back with a truck and hauls Clyde away.

The wind keeps blowing. The rain falls. At last, the days start to get a little longer, but there's mud everywhere. Once in a while, someone drives up with a busted trailer hitch or a boat part that needs to be welded, and I make a couple of dollars.

The only place I like to be is the shop. When I'm standing here holding the torch, lighting the torch, when I'm standing here making molten metal, putting pieces together, I feel whole. I love being out here. It's home.

BACK TO JERSEY

❧

Reuven nags me. He wants to meet his grandparents. Six years old—no father, no family. Can I go back? Can I see my parents? It's been almost ten years. What will it be like?

Okay, we'll go back to New Jersey, back to the world that doesn't know about freedom, love, justice—about the things I'm searching for.

My cousin Seymour picks us up at the airport. My parents meet us at the back door, me in a long skirt and backpack, Reuven in scruffy jeans and also a small backpack. The whole family is there to see us. My mother's cousin bends down to kiss Reuven. He turns his head away. She yells so everyone can hear, "He's not a kisser. He's not a kisser."

Ten days at my parents' house on Munn Avenue. We don't talk. My mother takes me shopping. "Put on some decent clothes," she says. When I do pick out something, she says, "No, not that—it's too expensive."

My father takes Reuven to his store, puts an apron on him, and shows him how to wait on the customers. Reuven likes the store, likes my father. He sits next to him at dinner. He wants to watch him shave in the morning. My father grills me. Am I working? What am I doing? Am I hanging out with those bad people? Am I taking care of Reuven? Am I spending too much money?

I don't belong here. I know that. I want to go home.

Reuven likes it here. He likes my father's store. He likes getting served meat, steak.

FIRE

❧

Smoke is pouring from underneath the tin garage. It's the middle of the night. Neighbors come knocking on the door to our house on Northwest Road. "Fire, fire, fire!" they yell. Smoke, smoke. My head is spinning.

Fire trucks, fire hoses smashing down the door, smashing down my fragile life, my dream of starting my own business—to do sculpture, do odd jobs, make some money, use the equipment, make the welds, feel the world that I've missed. Now it's going up in flames. Reuven and I stand there and watch. I hold his hand. The building burns. The firemen put out the fire, but there's not much left.

Cars come by the next morning. Biggy, Turk, others. "We heard about the fire.

Are you and Reuven all right?"

"Yeah, but we can't look inside."

"Aw, hell," says Biggy, "I'll go in."

"Me too," says Turk.

I follow them. Biggy opens the door. Smoke is coming out, but I can see clearly that the arc welding machine is scorched. Little bubbles of paint are on the outside of the Lincoln welder. Then I see the tanks, round tanks, the acetylene. The dials and knobs are black. Those I know not to touch, I know not to open them. The wood bench I made small stuff on is split in two and turned to charcoal. The vise is still standing, but when I get close I can see that the inside is messed up. The firemen are right. My shop is gone.

"No," says Biggy, "nothing much to save. We'll help you get it out of here."

Clyde is gone, the shop is burned down, the house is cold. On the weekend, we drive out to Wickersham, to Camilla and Kent's. Reuven can play with Scott and Michelle; I can talk to Camilla and have company. She serves me a bowl of lentil soup. When my stomach is warmed, she says, "Come on; we're going next door." Camilla with her small face framed in a big scarf and wearing a torn jacket walks out her front door, leaving me to follow. We walk across the muddy field. I've been here before. I know Skip. He came up here from California and bought forty acres to start a commune with Virgil, who grew up in the area.

Skip, standing in mud, says, "Hey, why don't you and Reuven move out here? The big house is empty. We're building a community—freedom, free place for kids to play, grow our own food. Fuck the system. This is where it's at."

I look at Skip. Blond, good-looking, long hair, long beard. I look at Camilla with her hands on her hips, her knowing way.

"Hey," Skip calls to Reuven, who's out in the field with Scott. "Come here, Reuven." He does. "Wanna live here, Reuven?"

Reuven looks around. "Sure."

"Okay, it's done. Yeah, there's a lot of folks living here. Wayne's in the dome. Penny and I are building a pyramid. Linda and Virgil have a cabin. Bob and Marion are building an A-frame, and Ube and Jack are back in the garage. The main house is empty. You can have it for twenty-five dollars a month."

Always looking for a better life, a better path, another way. It's never right; my life isn't right. I want out of Northwest Road. I'll go to Wickersham where there's hope, hope like I had on Northwest Road until I couldn't get in the firewood, until I couldn't take care of the animals, until I couldn't do it all alone. Here in Wickersham, I'll be with other people who have hope, who want to take a chance, who want to work together. Maybe I'll meet someone. Maybe I won't be alone—other people meet someone. There are guys out here—maybe, maybe.

New World Order

§

Spring 1972. We're sitting around the big old truck tire outside my rundown house that Skip has named the Mothership in Wickersham. Inhales, exhales. Skip passes the joint to Wayne, to Camilla, to Kent, to Bob, to Marion, to me, to Jack, to Ube. We're all here together now — Skip's college friend Wayne with a long red ponytail, bluegrass musicians Bob and Marion from California, Jack and Ube, locals who like the idea of making a community, Camilla and Kent, who have recently moved here, and me. Skip speaks between puffs.

"Hey, guys. We got all this land. We gotta make this place self-sustaining."

Wayne, "Yeah, we've talked about this before."

"Well, I got an idea, especially now that we got the tractor."

The tractor sits by the edge of the field. We all know the story. Barnes, down the road, told Skip if we wanted it, it was ours—we just had to get it off his land. A 1918 Allis-Chalmers, an old red tractor that actually works.

"We gotta plant something. We gotta have a crop out there in the field. Anyone with me here?"

"Sure, man."

More puffs.

"I know the farmers around here plant corn and stuff, but I've been doing a lot of reading, you know, and sunflowers are self-sustaining."

"Hey, man, what does that mean?"

"Aw, shut up. We got a good crop with sunflowers. They're not hard to grow and will make us some money."

"All right, man," says Kent, "let's go for it."

The guys drive down to Sedro Wooley to get seeds.

At the seed place, the guy says, "What are you going to do with all those seeds around here?"

"Oh, man, we're going to plant them."

"Plant them around here?"

"Yeah, that's what we're going to do."

"Okay, if that's what you want."

We all get the field ready. For three days, we turn the soil. It's time. We all get out there and put in the seeds, fifteen acres of sunflower seeds. Within a few weeks, the field is full of sprouting sunflower plants.

Hippie Seder

℘

It's spring in Whatcom County. There's mud all around, there are gray skies, and there are always hippies wanting a good meal.

Maybe it's seeing matzos at Everybody's Store near Deming. Maybe it's remembering that I haven't been to a Seder since I was a kid. Maybe it's the Women's Movement. I get the idea that I could put on a Seder, that a woman can put on a Seder. No more bearded grandpa from the old country. No more long nights listening to the men go on and on.

My friends, who have never heard of a Seder, say, "Sure, let's go for it."

No one has ever been to a Seder. No one knows what a Seder is.

"It's a big meal you have at Passover," I say. "It celebrates freedom—freedom for the oppressed, freedom from the pharaoh, freedom from, you know, the Establishment."

People say it's a cool idea. Camilla says we can have the Seder at her house.

I plan it, we all plan it. Lorna says she'll invite people. No one knows what to cook for a Seder. By now, everyone knows I can't cook.

"I'll get it together," I say. I call my mother. I call my cousin Sherry, who hasn't heard from me in years. They give me recipes—recipes for charoset, for maror, for karpas, and for all the other foods that are symbols of Passover.

The day of the Seder comes. I hand out the recipes to Camilla, Lorna, the other women. We have a lot of things to cook. I don't know how to cook. I don't know what I'm doing. "See you later," I say and take off.

I trudge across the muddy field, away from Camilla's house, away from the people gathering there, away from the Seder I planned. Why did I think I could put a Seder together?

After a while I go back.

"There she is," someone shouts. Lorna. "What do I do with this?" It's matzos that have to be soaked to make a kugel. I remember kugel. It's a casserole with apples and raisins and matzos. I look at the recipe and say, "Oh, we need to soak the matzos in hot water first."

I give directions to the women. I tell the guys to bring in some tables that are outside. We put them together to make one long table. Camilla has white linens. We put them on. I put the matzo on the table.

Lots of people show up. Not just hippies, people from around the valley. Here's Big Jeff, a guy from Brooklyn who owns Everybody's Store. The large room in Camilla's house fills up. There's Wayne, Skip and Penny, Lorna and Baloo, Bob and Marion, Kent and Camilla. And all the kids. Camilla is herding people to the table.

Big Jeff tells the story of the exodus from Egypt. We talk about freedom—Jews escaping from the pharaoh, hippies leaving suburbia. I teach everyone the "Dayenu," a Passover song I remember. We sing it. The kids sing with us. Michelle has just learned to read. We get her to tell the story of Passover. "Why is this night different from all other nights?" she begins.

She asks the four questions.

"Why on this night do we eat only matzo and not other bread?"

"Why on this night do we eat only bitter herbs?"

"Why on this night do we dip our herbs twice?"

"Why on this night do we eat only in a reclining position?"

This is beginning to look like the real thing. My grandfather led the Seder when I was a kid. I wasn't allowed to say a word. The women cooked, and the men sat around, praying and drinking wine.

Here we all drink wine. The kids run around playing. They run around, trying to find the *afikomen*—a piece of matzo that I hid under a bed. The finder gets a quarter. Someone passes another joint.

We need to eat. I start with the Hillel sandwich, not the way you usually start, but I'm hungry. I take a piece of matzo, put maror, bitter herbs that symbolize the bitterness of slavery, between the matzo, and bite down. Everyone follows. I look up. There're Skip and Penny, there's Kent, each holding up pieces of matzo, putting the maror in between. Camilla and Lorna made the charoset, the apples and almonds in wine and cinnamon. This symbolizes the mortar–Jews made bricks during slavery. A toke, a piece of matzo, another toke. I look up. Wayne, Scott, and Kent are biting down. I look up, I see smiles. More tokes.

Then the real meal. More food, more wine, more joints passed.

After dinner, guitars come out. Skip plays "If I Had a Hammer." We sing. We drink more wine, smoke more grass. We're full.

By the time people leave, it's dark. Everyone thanks me. "That was great," they say. "Let's do it again." For days people thank me. Around the valley, people know me as the chick who put on the Seder. I'm proud. For one day, I bring my two worlds together.

Square Dancing

❧

"Hey," Kent calls out as he stops by our house, "we're all going to Acme School tonight. There's a dance. Bring Reuven. We'll bring Scott and Michelle. It's some fundraiser."

"Oh, money." I look at Kent.

"That's all right. You don't have to give. We're bringing some vegetables from the garden."

Square dance. I can't dance. Lorna comes by. "Bob and I are going."

"Okay, okay," I say. "I'll go."

The night. We all pile into the truck on the farm. Two up front. A whole shitload of us in the back. The joints get passed. "Man," someone says, "if the locals are there, we better be cool." The truck stops on Turkington Road—near Highway 9—the lifeline for us getting in and out of the valley.

Tonight the school is lit up; tonight there are yellow and blue and green lights; tonight the gym is cleared except for the side tables of pretzels, cookies, and pop. Tonight I'm wearing a skirt—a plaid frilly skirt—something I never do. Tonight I'm wearing boots with toes that point, not my big work boots. Sylvia's got a ribbon in her long hair. Penny has a long flowing skirt. Camilla has a low-neck top. We are all here at Acme School. We gather round the caller—Norman.

We all know Norman, gray-haired, short-haired Norman. He's lived in Acme all his life.

I stare into the gym—I stare into the dance floor. Was it sixth grade I stood there and no one asked me to dance? I stood there hoping, praying someone would notice me, but no one did. I was the only one left without a partner. Mrs. Greenwald with her hair pulled tight in a bun came over and said, "Sit on the side. Maybe someone will ask you for the next dance." I knew better—I knew no one would ask me.

Now I'm in my skirt that moves around my high boots. Now I'm stoned, but I know no one will ask me. I watch for a while when the dancing begins. I watch Viviana throw her shoulders back and give a throaty laugh. I watch Penny staying close to Scott. I watch four guys in the corner who don't dance. Puff away on cigarettes. Standing, watching, not moving; this isn't for them. They walk out. I'm standing alone staring out at the dance floor.

I go outside. The guys are puffing on some weed. I go over to them, and one offers me a puff. I go inside. I see Reuven and Scott, curled up on a big pile of coats near the stage. I walk up and down. Take a pretzel, walk back and forth. I want to go home. I have to wait for the truck.

A big announcement, "Ladies and gentlemen, this is a big night. We're here to collect money for new playground equipment. We're glad to say we're close to meeting our goal—we're going to have some extracurricular activities for the kids. I look around. It's not only us from the farm; it's not only Lorna and Bob. It's all the local folks, the women dressed in soft-layered nylon dresses, the men in jeans, cowboy boots, and big belt buckles holding up their pants.

The caller, Norm, says, "We're all here for a good time. We don't want any inappropriate behavior, hear that?" What is he talking about? What is he saying? Inappropriate? Goddam them with their holier than thou attitude!

I just want to go home. Hours later, I pick up Reuven. Kent picks up Scott and Michelle. They're all asleep, and we make our way back on Highway 9 to Wickersham. I take Reuven inside, put him on the cot in the next room, go to the fridge. All I want to do is eat. All I want to do is not remember one more dance. I don't ever want to go to a dance again. I say that to myself over and over.

UBE

❧

Summer night. Camilla's. People talk and smoke, smoke and talk. Reuven is crashed with Scott and Michelle. I say goodnight to Camilla and slip out into the night. Behind me, the door opens. A patch of yellow light falls around me. The door closes, and the light disappears. Blackness. In the blackness I hear footsteps. I don't look back. I just walk. The footsteps gain on me.

"Hey," Ube falls in step beside me. We walk. I feel Ube looking at me. He's carrying his gun on his hip. I don't know why, but I'm attracted to him. I can't help it. I love his dark, slick hair, his craziness, his strong voice. I don't look at him.

"Follow me," he says in a gruff, no-nonsense voice.

I follow. We walk across the damp earth, under dark skies, a few stars overhead, our footsteps and the breeze the only sounds. We reach his garage hideout.

He pushes open the door. "Come in. Where the fuck are those candles?"

While he fiddles around for candles, I stand in the dark, in the cold. My body is stiff.

A match scratches flint. A bright flame springs to life. Ube lights a candle, blows out the match. In the dim light, I see rifles leaning on the corner, deer antlers nailed to the wall, a rough wooden table littered with machine parts and tools. I don't look at Ube.

"Come in back with me."

Small room. A bed heaped with blankets, a tiny bedside table with an ashtray. Cold and dark. My body stiff, unwilling to move. He sets the candle on the table and blows it out. Deep blackness. I want to run, but my body won't move. *I'm walking down the basement stairs. Frozen body. Frozen mind. Piles of boxes. Shadows and voices.*

"Lie down, woman," Ube commands, slapping the bed beside him. "Lie down."

The bedsprings creak. When Ube's finished, I lie in the dark, listening to his soft snoring, hearing the same voices I hear everyday, jumbled voices, men talking, men, whose voices I've heard everyday for as long as I remember. "*Don't say anything, little girl. Don't tell anyone or you'll get in big trouble. You're in trouble.*" I can't move. I can't think. I can only remember. Remember and wait. Wait for night to end and day to begin. Wait for the light to push away the darkness. Wait for the memories to leave me alone.

Later Ube gets up and gets dressed. "Gotta go," is all he says, and he's gone. The thoughts go around and around in my head. I want him. I want him to love me. I want him to be with me. Maybe this time someone will. Maybe Ube will.

REUVEN HITCHHIKING

❧

"I'll drive you to the Mount Vernon exit," I tell Reuven and his friend Willy.

Willy says, "I think Bellingham would be better. It's a bigger exit, and it's safer. We can always get off there if no one comes. We can walk into town."

I agree, "Okay, I'll drive you to Bellingham."

We load into the yellow VW bus. Reuven, age seven, and Willy, age eighteen, are going to hitchhike cross-country. Reuven wants to see his grandparents. He's been begging me to let him see his grandparents.

"I don't have that kind of money to send you," I tell him. I don't want him to see my parents. Tall, gangly, with stubble of a beard, blond, Willy's been hanging out at Camilla's house. I don't know where he showed up from, but he's there. He's friendly with the kids. I go over to Camilla's, and he's on the floor, playing Monopoly with Michelle by his side and Scott on the other side. I don't know how the plan is hatched, but Reuven and Willy decide to hitchhike cross-country, Reuven to see his grandparents and Willy to see the country. They tell me their idea. Actually, it's Reuven who wants to hitchhike. Willy says he'll go along.

"Groovy," I say. We figure out the best time to leave, morning. It's August—a good time of year, we think. It's Saturday morning. The night before they're going to leave, I help Reuven pack his little backpack that we got at the used store. We put one change of clothing in and some food—a quart of milk, some brownies, some tofu, some peanut butter, honey, and homemade bread sandwiches. A lot—we put a lot in for Reuven and another bag for Willy. I tell Reuven he'll need a jacket—it could get cold at night—so we get out his winter jacket. Too heavy to carry we decide. We get out a wool sweater and his nylon jacket, an extra pair of jeans and an extra pair of socks.

The long ride from Wickersham to Bellingham. I think it's great they're doing this. Wow, look at the opportunity my son's getting. We drive up to the exit. I get out of the VW, help them get things from the back, give a hug, and say good luck.

I drive away, leaving the seven-year-old and the eighteen-year-old by the side of the freeway with fifty dollars and Reuven's grandparents' address and phone number. I see them put their thumbs out as I drive away. For a moment I hesitate. What have I done? And then I think, "How groovy. I never had a chance like that." I drive back alone to Wickersham, the emptiness echoing through the VW van.

For three days, the house is quiet. There is no phone to call. I told Reuven to call Camilla's house collect if something goes wrong. No calls to Camilla. I begin to worry. Oh, my gosh, what if something happens to them?

A few days later, Camilla runs over and says, "Your father is on the line. He wants to talk to you. He said he would hold on."

Hold on? Something must be wrong. My father would never waste money like that. I drop what I'm doing and run over to Camilla's. My father, who is usually mild mannered and doesn't raise his voice, screams into the receiver, "What are you doing? We just got a call from Reuven—he's stranded in Atlanta. We wired money, and we got a plane ticket for him, and he's coming here. He says he wants to see us. Why didn't you tell me? I would have sent money."

"Oh, Dad, he wanted to go on this trip. He's with an older guy."

"You call eighteen older? And the guy said he had to leave, and Reuven is there by himself. You're lucky he didn't get kidnapped, young lady! He's tired and hungry. He'll be here tonight."

"Okay, have him call when he gets to your house. I'll wait by the phone."

Camilla says, "Go home and get a few things and just stay at my house." I do. I wait for the phone call. It comes.

"How are you?"

"Grandma and Grandpa are mad at you," Reuven says. "Real mad. They say you're crazy."

"Tell me about your trip," I say.

"We got rides all the way through. Just in Denver we had to wait for a long time. But it was cold in Chicago. And some guys in a real sports car drove us all the way through Wyoming at night. In the morning, they left us off and said they had to turn back. They said they wanted us to get through Wyoming—there's nothing there at night. Grandma and Grandpa give their dog steaks—real meat. I never get that. I'm gonna stay here for awhile."

"Okay," I say. "Call me on Saturday morning. I'll wait at Camilla's. I'll put Scott and Michelle on too. They're out getting wood now. Okay. Go get sleep."

"Okay."

Two weeks later, I drive down to Seattle to pick Reuven up at Sea-Tac Airport. He's still talking about how his grandmother feeds the dog steak.

WICKERSHAM HIGH

ℰ

I don't know how he shows up. He's just been here one day. Tall, dark, with wavy hair. A strong, well-built body. A friendly body. I'm thirty-one or so. He's twenty-two or so. His name is Bill.

"I've got some good stuff here. Ever take any?"

"No," I say.

"Want to?" he says.

"No," I say.

"This is good stuff. Won't do you any harm. Want to try?" he says. Again and again.

"No," I say.

"I'll tell you what, "he says. "Here, I'll slide a little, just put a little on your tongue. I'll do it too. It's not a lot. If nothing happens, we'll say, so what? If something happens, well, it won't be bad 'cause it's not a lot and it's real pure stuff."

"What about Reuven?" I say.

"He'll enjoy being around us, you'll see. It's the pure stuff. Here, just lick a little."

"A little, what's a little?" I think to myself, I'm the only one on the farm who hasn't taken LSD. I'm the only one who hasn't tripped. We sit there next to each other, waiting, waiting for the acid to take effect.

What will it be like? I sit there, waiting with Bill, and I don't know anything about him except that his mother is sick; she's away.

"Away where?" I say.

"In the hospital."

"What hospital?"

"I don't want to talk about it," he says.

The room turns slightly as the bright yellow from the gray window streams in, as the red hues from the ceiling light make shadows against his dark hair. Hair that follows the road, the road down the river, the river that has the spawning salmon, and he says, "Come lie by me." Or he comes to lie by me as the room moves to its own rhythm, as the voices stretch out to the hummingbird outside, the crackling of the fire inside, as I rise to put in another log.

I move sideways against the crate that's now the table in the room where we're sitting, and I feel light, the light from within, the light above, and Bill feels warm and nice, and his soft body becomes a safe place. We lie together upstairs in a room with a single bed and nothing else. We lie together, watching the red lights, the blue, soft blue, the yellow, bright yellow, and I don't see my kid. I don't see anything for three days as we lie there, swarmed by light, both the inner and outer. We lie there.

Our bodies come together, and it's soft, and he whispers to me, and I whisper back, for three days. Reuven comes in and out during the three days. He likes Bill. They talk about cars and trucks, about getting wood, about motorcycles in between the light coming through, in between the bodies coming together. They talk, and Reuven says, "I'm going to Scott's." We don't get up for three days, and then Bill wakes up from the sleep we're in and says, "Maybe I better go."

I say, "Will I see you again?"

And he says, "I'll always see you, beautiful one."

The light dims into night.

"I better find Reuven," I say.

And he kisses me goodbye and says goodbye again, and we stand there in the embrace, bathed in the light of the world, and he says he needs to see his mother in the hospital, and we say goodbye again, and I go to take a shower.

I want him to stay, but he says he isn't ready to be a father. He says he'll come see me.

Father. The word cracks me open. My father has disappeared from my being these three days with the light coming in. The days, the nights, I am a young woman whose body carries her through, and the ghosts of my life lie still for just that time—so still I can't even feel it anymore. Oh, the beauty of the sun coming through the glass, lying next to Bill, my body warm all over. It stays warm until he walks out the door, and I scream inside, don't leave, and he says he has to.

Why? Why does he have to leave? The ghosts return, my father in his jockey underwear answering the door, my quiet father who hovers over me is here again, and I don't know where to go from Wickersham where the rain comes through the glass panes and the water seeps in through the floor, where there isn't any place but the damp house with broken plumbing, and I know I need to get out of there. I need to find Bill, but I have no idea where he lives. His body is no longer warm beside me. I'm alone in the night, shivering under the thin covers, trying to get up to feed the fire and keep the house going out here in Wickersham.

Reuven Starts School

§

It's Saturday. Reuven is outside, splitting wood with his small axe. I come out the back door. He puts down the axe. "I want to go to school," he says, "real school like the other kids."

"Scott and Michelle don't go to school."

"Yeah, but the other kids do. I want to go to school. I want to go on the school bus."

"Okay, finish splitting the kindling and stack it inside, and I'll think about it."

He doesn't pick up the axe. "No, I want to go to school."

"Well, you can't go today. It's Saturday. I promise I'll find out about it."

Why does he want to go to school? It's stupid, stifling. He's not going to learn anything. My mind swirls. Should I let him go? Camilla and Kent wouldn't let their kids go. It's corrupting. We've all been corrupted. I shouldn't expose him to that world.

He keeps badgering me all weekend, so on Monday morning, I put on my overalls, plaid shirt, boots and walk into Acme Elementary School. Except for the square dance, I haven't been in an elementary school since I was at Hillside Avenue. They look similar—old brick buildings, smelly halls, institutional paint on the walls, tall windows. I walk into the administrative office, ask for the principal. The secretary asks what I need. She's got teased blond hair, a short skirt, high-heeled boots. I tell her I want to find out about enrolling my son in school.

"How old is he?" she asks.

"Seven, and he's never been to public school," I boast.

"Wait here," she says.

The principal comes out. He's wearing a dark suit, dark tie, white pressed shirt. I haven't seen anyone in Wickersham in a suit, ever. Oh no, I think. What am I going to do? The principal looks me over, from my work boots to my long dark hair, from bottom to top.

"What can I do for you?" he says.

"My son wants to go to school, so I'm here to enroll him."

"You need to have his previous school send his transcripts."

"Transcripts?" I say. "He's never been to public school. He went to the Bellingham Co-op School for a while, but they don't give grades.

"Oh, well, we'll put him in second grade. Has he had his inoculations?"

"Sure," I say, although I don't have any record of the shots he got in California.

"Okay, bring him in tomorrow, and we'll put him in. And please, give him a bath tonight."

That bastard.

I go home. I tell Reuven he can start tomorrow. He's excited. I tell him I'll take him tomorrow, but after that he can get the school bus on the road. "You've got to get up by yourself and be ready when the bus comes at 7:15 a.m.

"Okay, I'll do that." He runs over to tell Scott and Michelle he's going to school.

When Reuven starts school, I don't ask him about homework, about activities. "How was school?" I say.

"Fine," he says.

"Please bring in some wood before you do anything else." He does.

I need to change my name. Reuven has started school. His last name is Carlisle, the same as his father's. My last name is Waldman. In Whatcom County where everyone with children is married and there are no divorces, we have different last names. Okay, I'm going to change our names. I think of all kinds of names that are common for hippies: Freedom, Love, River, Sky. Joan River, Joan Sky, Reuven River, Reuven Sky.

"No," Reuven says. "I don't want those names."

I don't know what to do. I ask Melissa—activist, bright Melissa. She knows. "Use Carlisle," she says, "but change the spelling to Carlyle. That's the Welsh way, not the English. Then, the father can't make trouble."

Okay. Melissa says she'll do the paperwork. We go before a judge. Reuven is too young to go. It's just me. Standard questions. "Why are you changing your name?"

"Because I want my son and me to have the same last names, so I'm changing them both."

A big stamp. Case dismissed. Carlyle. My name is Joan Carlyle. Reuven's is Reuven Michael Carlyle. Michael—he chooses this name. He wants a more common name. Corsa is erased—his father's family name. Carlisle is erased. One side is erased—with a stamp.

Before Thanksgiving, I get a call from Reuven's teacher. "Mrs. Carlyle," she says, "can you come in tomorrow? I would like to talk to you."

"Sure," I say. I go. We sit down. Me, this time in a long patchwork skirt and loose top and sandals with wool socks. She, in a blue polyester suit and low black heels.

"Mrs. Carlyle, this is what we are working on. This is Reuven's class work. The problem is he can't read, and he's in second grade, so he's very far behind. We would put him in first grade, but we don't have any room in first—no room at all. We don't know what to do. I've tried tutoring him, but he's too far behind.

I'm in shock. I had no idea he couldn't read.

"Can I get tutoring for him?" I ask.

"Of course, you can arrange intensive tutoring."

"Okay, how much does it cost?"

"The usual cost is ten dollars an hour."

"Well, it's a lot of money, but I'll see about getting it."

"We have several names. You can see who you like and who is available. I would suggest after school and weekends."

"Okay, okay."

I walk out. How come they didn't call me before? He's been there almost two months. I'm pissed, real pissed, but I get the tutor. Reuven stays up late and practices his reading, and after two months, we're all amazed that he's up to grade level.

School. I don't go to PTA meetings. I don't help with schoolwork, but now I do ask if he's done his homework.

WOMEN AND THEIR MEN

❧

September 1972. I climb into my VW bus. I need to get food. We buy food in bulk—one-hundred-pound bags of brown rice, durum wheat flour, oats. I always have errands. I ride around. My mother rode around. She couldn't stand staying at home.

The VW bus coughs, sputters, catches. I rev it up until it's warm enough to drive, then let out the clutch and bump along. At the end of the long dirt driveway, I turn left onto Highway 9 and look back at the cold, damp house and soggy, broken field that surrounds it like a mud moat.

I drive past neat red farmhouses set back from the road. Pickup trucks in front, chicken coops to the side, barns out back, tractors in the field. It's fifteen miles to Bellingham. The road is black and wet from last night's rain. The tires of my VW bus hiss on the wet asphalt.

I'm in town. I go to the co-op on Harris Avenue. It's just a few blocks from the shipyard. Pete's working there; Mike's working there. I look down the block. I can't help it. I've got to pass by.

I stop the VW. I park and walk into the office.

"Can I please speak to Leonard?"

He's the foreman. I've been asking for Leonard now once a week for almost a year. The office staff knows me. "Leonard to the office," I hear over the loudspeaker. Leonard walks up the stairs in his coveralls, holding his hardhat.

"Leonard," I say, "can I have a job?"

"Sorry," he says. "We don't have any openings."

We go through this ritual every week. I won't give up. This time, though, I walk out, and I'm crying. I can't stand it anymore. Pete sees me as I walk by.

"Hi, Joan."

"Hi, Pete."

Why can't I be there with him and Mike? Why can't I weld? Why?

The shipyard. What is it about the shipyard that's home? I feel at home walking with the men, walking with Pete. I feel at home with the cranes overhead, with the smell of steel all around me, with the tap of the rod, with the sparks of fire. It is home. It was home when I worked at Hunter's Point.

The shipyard feels like a different kind of home.

I've got to get Leonard to hire me. It's almost four thirty. I'll go up and meet Pete and Mike—they're usually at the Fairhaven Tavern after work. I wait. Pete, with his quick step and quick smile, motions for a drink and sits down. Mike follows.

"Pete, I gotta get a job. I can't stand it. I want to weld. I want to be working with you guys."

"Yeah, it's bum deal," he says. "Leonard says they're going to need some guys in a few weeks. We'll see. How's Reuv doing?"

"Okay, I guess."

"I should come out to see him."

There are peanut shells on the floor of the tavern. Pete has had his daily beer, and so has Mike. I don't even pretend to drink. Just want to eat those peanuts. They wave goodbye, and I drive the VW back to Wickersham.

It's dusk when I get home. The house is cold and dark and empty. I'm too tired to start a fire, too tired to cook. I go back out into the fading light and walk across the gray, muddy field to Camilla's.

The house is full of people. Two guys are sitting on the sagging green sofa, a few more are stretched out on the floor, talking and laughing. The air is thick with pot smoke. Camilla hands me a huge bowl of lentil soup.

I stand in the doorway between the kitchen and the living room. Penny, Lorna, and Camilla sit at the kitchen table. Camilla has her yarn out. She's crocheting a hat for Scott. Lorna has sewing with her, too. She's sewing patches onto Jason's pants. Penny is holding a cigarette and talking.

"I just planted yesterday," she says. "Skip tilled the garden, and I put in the zucchini and beans. Couldn't wait any longer. I don't know how long we'll be here, but I want a garden."

"What do you mean?" says Camilla. "You thinking about going somewhere?"

"Oh, I don't know. It's just hard being out here with little Nicki. I think about moving back into town, but Skip won't hear of it. This is his dream."

"I hear you," says Lorna, her thin body shivering. "I can't stand that old goat herder's tent we're living in. I just want our house to be finished." She talks about the house Bob is building. Says it's going to be a rustic octagonal Victorian with a turret and cone-shaped roof.

"How creative," says Camilla.

"That's my Bob," Lorna says. "This house is his vision. That's what I admire about him."

They sew and talk about their men. I watch. I listen. I shuffle my feet around. I don't say anything.

The men laugh and smoke joints. "Fuck Nixon," they say. "Fuck the government. Fuck this stupid war. Fuck the money-grubbing capitalist machine." They say they want to live off the land.

I stand in the doorway between kitchen and living room. Between the men and the women. Between men talking about a new world order and women talking about their men. I watch and listen. I stare at the floor; I stare at the ceiling. I don't say anything. I thought I would have a home at the commune, but I don't belong here.

BORN AGAIN

֍

It's Sunday morning. Lorna's talked me into going to church with her. Every time I go over to see Lorna she tells me, "You've got to come to church with me. I've found God, and you can too. It's the best thing that's ever happened to me."

"But Lorna," I say, "I'm not Christian; I'm Jewish."

"It doesn't matter," she answers. "You'll feel God. A lot of people in the valley go."

"Okay."

This Sunday is a special Sunday. The pastor has invited a special healing minister from Vancouver.

Lorna picks us up in her old Ford truck. Reuven and Lorna's son, Jason, climb into the back. I'm wearing clean black pants from the local thrift store and a clean pullover black top. Usually I wear the same jeans every day. Lorna's wearing her Sunday best. We both have on work boots as it's muddy around the area.

We drive up to a small brick building with a steeple on top. I've passed this church so many times on my way into town, but it's always been quiet. Now I see families going in.

I hope this isn't a mistake.

We park the truck in the church parking lot. Jason and Reuven jump out the back and disappear. Lorna and I walk in. There are no empty seats on the main floor, so we go to the side balcony. I'm amazed this little church can fit so many people.

"Oh, no," I say to myself. Polyester. All I see is women in polyester with sprayed-down hair.

Reuven and Jason find us. Reuven whispers into my ear, "Everyone in my class is here."

Stares. Eyes are on us. Mothers whispering to each other. No one comes up to Lorna and me; no one extends a hand to me as a newcomer.

The service begins. A choir. Music comes from behind us. The pastor gets up, introduces the one from Vancouver, and they both put their hands in the air, shouting, "Almighty," again and again. "Almighty, Almighty," and then people are moving up to the front, and the one from Vancouver with big hands and the loud voice takes over, and the people are swaying and singing, "Almighty, Almighty," as they walk, and then one falls to the floor and another, and they writhe about and more people go up. Now Lorna is downstairs, moving around, too. I just want to run out.

Reuven and Jason are gone. I can't move. I just sit there, and suddenly the pastors say, "We thank you, Lord. We thank you, Lord." And one says to give money, it's God's will for us to enjoy the fruit of his being. A basket is passed around. I just want to get out of here. I never want to see these people again. I want to go home.

"Lorna, let's get out of here," I say.

She says, "Oh no, this is part of the service. Let God in."

"Oh God, just let me out," I pray. After the service is over, Lorna and I never talk about it again.

A few weeks later, in late October, Reuven's teacher calls me.

"Mrs. Carlyle, I have to tell you something," she says. "We had a mock election in class today. Reuven and I were the only ones who voted for McGovern. All of his classmates voted to re-elect Nixon."

I thank her for letting me know. Born-again and Nixon country. I've got to get out of here.

NOT MY DREAM

❦

I wake up to a cold house. Again. Three people crashed on the floor. I step over bodies to get to the kitchen.

This isn't what I expected. I didn't think I would be living with gun-toting guys who smoked dope all the time and didn't give a damn. But here I am again. Alone. Alone in the rundown Mothership, alone with Reuven, alone with no fire, no bathroom, no running water.

Thoughts chase each other through my head. Where am I going to get wood? When am I going to get food? Why don't I have any money? Why doesn't anyone like me?

I turn on the faucet and nothing comes out. No water today. I'll have to get some from the well and heat it up on the stove.

The bathroom door is open. Nothing in there works either. A month ago, I woke up to find that the floorboards under the big white clawfoot bathtub had rotted through and given way. The tub sits there like a sinking ship, its stern still on the floor, its bow resting on the dirt below. I asked Skip, with his persuasive smile, if he could fix it.

"Sure, cool, no problem," he said.

He never showed up, so I asked Kent, Camilla's husband, standing there with his tall, lean frame. He gazed at the sunken tub, scratched his beard, "Yeah, I'm sure I can do something about that."

A week later, I asked Wayne, big Wayne with the long red ponytail.

"A cinch," he said. "All we gotta do is patch in a handful of new floorboards. Hammer, nails, saw, boards."

Another two weeks gone, and the tub is still sunk. I still can't light a fire, much less fix a sunken bathtub.

Today it's cold even with the sun out. I grab a wool shawl and trudge to the paved road to the rusty metal mailbox, which a bunch of us share. I wait for the mailman so I can get my welfare check before someone else picks up the mail. I don't want my check to end up wet and dirty on the floor of someone's teepee, lost behind a backpack or stack of books. I thought we were going to take care of each other.

I've got to get out of here. I've got to get to Bellingham to cash my check. It's fifteen miles to the co-op. The people at the co-op cash my check. One hundred forty-two dollars. It will have to last the month.

When I get home in the afternoon, I see greasy-haired Ube by the side of the house chopping wood. Reuven is beside him. Next to Ube, he looks so small and skinny with his brown and white plaid shirt that's two sizes too big, covered with wood chips. When Reuven sees me, he holds up the big axe, proud, so I can see what he's doing.

"Get some of these bags," I shout. "I can't carry them all myself."

Reuven looks in the burlap grocery bags. "Did you buy any cookies?"

"Yeah, but you can't have any now. You eat too much junk."

He takes a jug of milk and a box of Cheerios out of the bags.

"Do you have to eat that everyday? Can't you eat something else once in a while? And I don't want you eating anything till after there's a fire going."

Reuven puts down the box of Cheerios and runs out and gets kindling. He goes out a second time and comes back with a couple of split logs.

"I helped Ube make these," he says.

I don't answer.

I ball up some newspaper, stack kindling on it, and use a wooden matchstick to light around the edges. Smoke pours out the stove door, burns my eyes.

"Dammit."

Ube walks in. "Girl, you need to learn how to make a fire."

"Show *him*," I say, nodding toward Reuven.

Ube gets on his knees, and Reuven stands beside him, hands on knees, leaning forward, peering into the stove. "You start by twisting the paper tight," Ube instructs. "See? You make little paper logs." Soon a fire is crackling, and warmth spreads through the living room.

Ube hangs around, smokes a joint. When he figures out I'm not going to cook anything, he ambles away into the late afternoon.

Dusk comes on. A little light is left above the horizon, between the mountains they call The Sisters. I'm hungry.

"Come on," I tell Reuven. "We're going to Camilla's. Bring some clean clothes. We can take a bath."

We make our way across the field in the ghostlike gloom. The smell of soup reaches us through the door. There's a big pot of it on the stove, and brown rice.

"Help yourself," Camilla yells. "It's white bean soup." She gets out tin bowls and beat-up spoons from the free store and sets them on the table.

"Reuven needs a bath," someone says.

"Fine. He can take one with Scott," Camilla says.

I wolf down two bowls of soup. "I've got to get back. It's really cold in that house—I don't want the fire going out on me."

Walking down the muddy path, my mind won't stop. What's going to happen to us? I've got to get out of here—the dreams are dead, flat dead. The sunflower crop failed. The wet fields, the wet world out there—the plants drooped. We picked out the seeds of the good ones. We cleaned them. We gathered about a hundred of the best plants. All those plants and maybe we had ten pounds. Then Skip tried to sell them. Ten pounds. We were laughed at. There was no market for sunflowers. Locals came by, shaking their heads. We didn't ask the local farmers. We didn't know. They knew corn is the crop for the wet Northwest, not sunflowers.

There are no dreams left. There is no life left. I don't belong here. I need to get to Bellingham. I need to get away from here. Wickersham. It isn't my dream. The only dreams I have are nightmares. I can't plant. I can't sew. I can't farm. I can't cook. I can't love.

I can work. I am a trained welder.

PART 5

&

STANDING STRONG

THE TEST

&

October 1972. "Come in Friday to take the test," says Leonard, the short, stocky foreman at Fairhaven Shipyard.

Yikes! How did this happen? Every week for a year, I've come here and asked for a job. Every week Leonard has said no. I wait till Pete gets off work. He tells me, "Mike and I threatened to walk out if he didn't hire you."

The yard. It sits at the end of Harris Avenue, overlooking Bellingham Bay.

I walk into the yard. Leonard takes me over to a metal-frame open building. It has a corrugated metal top—no sides. The wind is blowing. It's raining, not a downpour but that wet Northwest rain, spraying mist all over. I'm wearing my work boots. I'm wearing leather coveralls and a bib jacket. I carry my helmet and gloves.

"This is Tom. He'll show you how to set up," says Leonard. I see power saws, power grinders. I see vises. I see arc welders. I see a handful of other workers standing around staring at me.

"Get back to work," Tom yells out to them.

"You might want to practice a while before you start," he tells me. "Get a feel for the equipment. Here's the scrap bin. Here's the 1017 rods you can use. We need a horizontal, overhead, and vertical weld. Got it? It should take an hour, but you can practice for a while."

Quiet noise surrounds me as I sit down. The noise of the buzzers, the saws, the grinders. The quiet of no other workers in my area, the quiet of stares from afar in the big open space with the sound of raindrops coming off the metal. I shiver, and I go to the bin, take out scrap pieces. I'm shivering from the cold, but the sweat is coming down my forehead.

I flip down my hood. The rod feels strange. I strike an arc. I start laying beads. I know I'm being watched, and I'm nervous. I have to do it right. I lay bead after bead, get more scrap metal from the bin, keep welding. I've never had to do it perfectly, to test the welds to see if they crack. I can't fail now. I've waited so long. If I mess up, I won't be able to weld.

I love the smell of the yard, the smell of the flux powder, the smell of the grinders, the smell of the machines—big machines, small machines. I love the feel of the yard. It's big. It's open. I've got to work here. I stare at the three-quarter-inch plates. I touch the torch. I know that a guy would just come in and run a few practice plates, call the foreman over and say, "I'm ready."

I work through the lunch hour. Tom comes over, "How ya doing? Want to give it a try?"

"I'd like to practice a little longer."

"Okay, come get me when you're ready."

I get up and reach for another plate, strike up an arc, and practice the vertical.

I stare at the plates.

I stare out at the yard.

I stare at the world in front of me.

At two forty-five, Tom comes by. "Closing is at four. Here're some clean plates. You better start."

I slide my helmet over my face. I set up the plates. First, I do the overhead. I strike the arc and just keep my hand moving. I do all three positions, overhead, vertical, and flat.

"All right, Carlyle," he says, "we'll give them the test."

Tom picks up my three pieces with pliers. They're hot. He immerses them in water and brings them over to a machine to bend them. No cracks.

"All right, Carlyle," he says, "sit here.

Leonard comes back with Tom and says, "All right, you pass. Start Monday."

I walk out—soot on my face, my arms are numb. Pete and Mike are waiting for me. "Let's go up to the Fairhaven Tavern and get a drink."

Other workers ignore us, watch us walk out. Pete, short, dark haired, who likes his drinks, puts his arm around me. "You made it. I'll show you around on Monday."

I can't believe I've been hired—after begging for a job week after week. How am I going to work out the logistics? Reuven and I are living in Wickersham—still in the Mothership that's still falling apart. I can't commute back and forth every day. It's too much. An hour and a half each way.

I go over to Camilla's. "Can Reuven stay at your house during the week? I'll be back Friday night."

"Sure," she says.

I get ready to leave early on Monday morning. On Sunday night, I give Reuven detailed instructions. "Go next door to Camilla's after school and stay there for the week. You can come home and get your clothes, but sleep at Camilla's."

He promises. I know he'd rather be with Scott and Michelle than alone with me anyway. We'll make it work.

Setting Up

§

I drive my yellow VW bus down to the shipyard, grab my new red toolbox, and walk to the administration building. Leonard sees me.

"Follow me. We're going to put you out here."

We cross the yard where ships are waiting for repair. "This is Randy, your boss," he says, leading me to a burly man, holding a big wrench and a long sheet of metal.

Randy eyes me up and down. "You want work; you got it. Give these guys a hand." He disappears.

I don't know what we're working on, but the first few days, Pete says, "Stay close to me." I do, but I don't see him welding. I see him walking up and down ladders, carrying metal from one place to another, carrying wood planks from one place to another. Pete walks back and forth. So does Mike. They stop. They chat. They take out a measuring tape. I can't figure out what is going on. Oh, I hope they don't fire me for standing around. We're not doing anything—no welding. Won't we get fired?

"What's going on?" I ask Pete.

"It's called setting up so we can weld. You have to put the pieces in place."

"But aren't we going to get docked for spending all this time?" I wonder.

No one is welding. Others are walking back and forth also. We make a platform of wood planks so that we can stand on it and weld. I get up and do my first overhead welding. I get up there and feel my hand moving along. I don't get it, though. We're being paid for setting up. Sometimes it takes a day or so.

Tools. My co-workers reach for a tool, a come-along. I've never heard of it—I've never seen one before. It pulls the metal together. "Here," Mike says, "give it a try."

A whistle blows. Five-minute break. Cigarettes come out. Guys congregate in small groups, smoking. I go up to Leonard.

"Where's the restroom?"

"Down there." He points to the administration building way down the yard. "You gotta use theirs. There's no ladies' room around here."

I make the long walk and go into the administration building, feeling real conspicuous. In the ladies' room, a secretary with teased blond hair stands in front of the mirror, putting on bright red lipstick. She stares at me—at my dirty hands, my dirty face, my disheveled hair, my heavy leather work gear.

"What are you doing here? This ain't your bathroom."

"There's no ladies' room out in the yard. They told me to use this one."

I'm mad. They knew I was coming. Couldn't they have set up a bathroom? Now I have to walk a quarter-mile every time I need to go to the bathroom.

The yard has its routine. Work starts at seven. I drive my VW bus into the yard. I don't have to change like at Hunter's Point. I'm wearing my leather pants and jacket. I'm carrying my helmet and red toolbox. I drop off my lunch. Posters of nude women stare down at me from the lunchroom wall. The guys come in with their black lunch pails. I have a soft blue lunch box from the sporting goods department.

The first few days in the lunchroom, the guys are cordial. They don't say much. The talk goes over my head. I bring salads in a plastic container. I stare at their big sandwiches on whole wheat or white bread. I stare at their zucchini bread. All homemade food. I notice their pants, always clean, always freshly laundered. I don't have someone to make me zucchini bread or do my laundry. Sometimes I wear the same pants a few days in a row. I'm just too tired to do laundry when I get home.

SCAFFOLD

❧

A few days later, I'm up on a scaffold, welding rod in hand. There's loud noise all around—buzzing power saws, whirring grinders, squealing train wheels, clanging metal. The shipyard is humming, charged with energy. We're out in the open, smelling the sea, sulfur, and burning metal. Pete shows me how to get started, how to finish the bead, how to grind the weld smooth. When he leaves, it's just me and my tools. I strike an arc, lay my first bead, weld.

All afternoon I weld and grind, grind and weld. Under the leather coat and leather pants and leather gloves, I begin to sweat. I don't slow down. I have to keep pushing. At two thirty, we get a five-minute break, then it's steady welding till the whistle shrieks again at four thirty.

At home I peel off my gear and slip into the bathtub. My legs are sore. My back aches. I doze off, jerk awake. For dinner I have leftover rice and beans. I'm in bed by nine o'clock, but so exhausted I can't fall asleep. I lie in bed and worry–that I'm not strong enough, that the hours are too long, that I'll never be a good welder. I worry that I don't have anyone to make my lunch, put dinner on the table when I get home, wash my work clothes. I worry about the men, their crude comments, their crude suggestions. When the alarm clock jolts me awake at 6:00 a.m., I feel like I've hardly slept, but at 6:50, I'm in work gear, driving down Harris Avenue with my helmet and red toolbox on the seat beside me.

For the next few days, I'm up on a big, wide scaffold, welding long rows of metal sheet. I flip down my hood, grip the rod, strike an arc, make fire. My hand moves along, sparks fly, metal softens.

Each time I flip down my hood, for a moment I slip into the darkness. I go underground. Here, under the hood, I'm in the dark, and I can feel the steel of the ship hull in front of me. I hear from inside, *See what we have here, Joe, the boss's daughter. Hold her, Joe, I'm coming in.* This darkness I know so well.

The moment passes, and I feel the rod in my hand. I strike an arc, and a hot white fire splits the darkness, shooting red and yellow sparks into the air. Metal softens and melts, pieces of steel come together, fused into a single unbreakable piece. I make weld after weld, bringing light to the darkness, bringing separate things together. I feel alive with the torch in my hand. I feel at home.

On the way to lunch, I pass a couple of men.

"Go home, lady," one of them snarls. "You don't belong here."

"You're taking a job away from a man," the other hisses.

Leonard intercepts me outside the lunchroom. "The secretaries are complaining," he says. "They said you're making a mess of the ladies' room. Can you try to be a little more careful?"

"Then find a bathroom for me around here somewhere."

"Can't. Regulations. Just be more careful."

Friday comes. The whistle shrieks at four thirty, and my first week is over. I walk out of the yard weary but relieved, knowing I have a lot of things to learn if I want to keep this job. I'll have to learn how to use all the tools—the bench grinder, come-along, drill press, spud wrench, chipping gun. I'll have to learn carbon arc and electroslag welding and how to weld a smooth butt joint, lap joint, corner joint, edge joint, and T joint. I'll have to swallow my fears and climb up the ladder all the way to the top girders. I'll have to learn to put up with guys who have Nixon bumper stickers on their pickup trucks, go hunting on weekends, and say I need a good fuck and real food.

I also know this job is for me. I love the smell of welding—the molten steel, the cool air that sweeps through the yard. But mostly it's the welding I love–striking the arc and laying the bead, bringing separate pieces of steel together into a solid, unbreakable whole. I want to do this more than I've ever wanted to do anything.

Reuven, the Bachelor

≈

It's Friday afternoon, the end of my first week at the shipyard. I drive back to Wickersham after work. I'm exhausted and can't wait to get home and in bed.

I open the door and see Reuven making a peanut butter sandwich. I see wood chips, clothes, games, dirty bowls, bread and cereal crumbs all over the living room.

"Reuven, what are you doing here? You're supposed to be at Camilla's."

He looks at me, puts his head down.

I yell, "What are you doing here? You're not supposed to be here."

He's holding the peanut butter jar with one hand while trying to spread peanut butter with the other. This small blond boy with denim overalls looks up at me and says very slowly, "I'm practicing to be a bachelor."

I want to burst out laughing. "What do you mean 'I'm practicing to be a bachelor?' Reuven, did you stay here at night? Did you stay here all week?"

He nods.

I can't believe it. How did this happen?

"You were supposed to go to Camilla's. Didn't you go?"

He shakes his head no.

"Didn't Camilla come and check up on you?"

He shakes his head. "I just wanted to be here. I told her."

"You stayed here all week?"

I can't believe it.

"Come on, "I say. "We're going into town. We're going to have to move to Bellingham. You can't stay out here all week being a bachelor. We're moving to town."

INITIATION

§

Three of us are working near the bow of a ship. It's a windy day, and sparks are blowing all around as we work. Just as I flip up my hood, a few big sparks blow right down the inside of my leather jacket, against my skin. They burn my bare breasts. I scream and throw down my rod. The other two guys watch, aghast, as I beat at my chest and squirm and tear at my clothes, screaming the whole time. Finally the sparks fall out, still burning. My eyes water. I want to cry, but I don't. My supervisor, Randy, pulls out the first-aid kit and hands me some salve. I take it and head for the ladies' room. Half an hour later, I'm back at work. Randy says, "Well, you've had your initiation. Welcome to the club. We all have our scars."

The next day I'm setting up, and Randy comes by. "Carlyle," he says, "tack these parts here before you begin welding."

I quickly realize that I have to move the tanks over, the oxyacetylene tanks. Fordy and Jim have been carrying tanks back and forth all morning. I look around, and there are none near me now. Fordy, a loud-talking local, is standing a few yards away from me. I walk over to him, my chipping hammer hitting against my side as I walk. He's welding, and I look away so I don't get a flash. I wait until he finishes and calmly ask, "Could you please move the tanks over for me?"

He looks at me. Doesn't say a word. Picks up one heavy tank, throws it on his shoulder, walks past me, and keeps walking until he gets to my station. He sets the tanks down and heads back. He says, "Carlyle, you are a pain in the ass." He then gets the other tank and sets it down. I'm walking back now, and on his way back, we cross paths.

He doesn't look at me. I say, "Thanks, Fordy."

"You owe me one, lady."

"All right, I'll buy you a drink later."

"You owe me more than that."

I go back to my station, put on the goggles, and start tacking.

THE PROVIDER: LAYING THE FIRST WELD

❧

February 1973. The shipyard gets a contract to build a 120-foot Alaska king crab boat, bound for the Bering Sea. I've been working at the yard for a few months. I've learned to run beads outside. I've learned how to use a come-along. I've learned to expect nasty remarks. Up till now, we've had small jobs, repairing and working on small boats.

All week, I hear talk about starting the boat, the *Provider*, about what a plum contract it is, about how we're going to have a lot of work. Randy, my boss, comes up to me. "Carlyle, we want you to lay the first weld. Next Monday is the big day." I look at him, mouth open, not believing his words.

"Oh, it's nothing," he says. "Just tack the long pieces of steel laid out. We thought you would like the honor." Like the honor? Of course, I would! But can I do it? What if I can't strike the arc? What if the guys laugh at me? What if?

All week, there's preparation. The yard is cleared by the water. Old scrap metal, old tools, leftover equipment—it's all taken away. Long pieces of metal are laid out.

On Monday, the whistle blows, and all work stops. The workmen, the secretaries gather around the empty yard with the long pieces of metal laid out. The mayor is there, local businessmen are there. Men in suits. There are speeches about economic growth in this small town. Congratulations to Helge, the owner. Leonard motions for me to come forward. I have my helmet beside me, my leathers fastened, the rope leading to the welding machine over my shoulder. Leonard points to the steel. I walk over. I don't shake, I don't cry. I'm numb. All eyes are watching me. I flip down my hood and strike an arc. Sparks fly, the metal gets molten, and I weld the two long pieces of steel together. The ship's owner, Helge smashes a bottle of champagne, and everyone cheers.

The celebration ends, and Leonard motions for everyone to get back to work. I pick up the torch and start welding.

HANGING ON

ℬ

"Carlyle, weld up there today." Randy, my boss, points his finger up. We've been working almost round the clock on the *Provider*. We've welded the steel base, and now most of the work is being done up high—the house, the rafters. I look up. It's high. I go to the ladder. Mark and John are already up there. I take my leads, I take my helmet, I take my chipping hammer, and I start the climb. Rain—light rain starts. Oh, no. I want to cry. I want to go home. No one sees the tears coming down my face. When I get to the top, I look down, and I want to throw up. I say to myself, "Don't look down."

I position myself, holding on with one hand, holding my torch in the other, and I start welding. The raindrops come off my hood. Mark yells over to me, "Hang on tight." No kidding! How am I going to do this? What time is it? Lunch? How can I last until lunch? I make a bead. I chip away the slag. I make another bead. I know I shouldn't look down. I do. I see Leonard and Randy. They look so small. I realize one wrong move, and I could fall. I keep welding. I finish a whole section. The whistle blows. It's lunch. I slowly climb down. John and Mark are already down. "It's a bitch up there in the rain," I hear. They walk together to the Quonset hut. I follow, the tears still on my face.

"Hey, Carlyle, you wanna be a welder? Well, you got it. We're gonna be up high there for a few weeks." I want to bolt out. A few weeks. I can't take it—up there for hours, holding on for dear life.

The buzzer rings—loud. Lunch is over. I slowly walk back. The rain has stopped—just moist air. I climb up again. Mark says, "Hold on. We have only three and a half hours left." I give him a slight smile. I don't know if he is being kind to me or if he is making fun of me, if he knows that I feel like a fraud. What am I doing here? Hanging from the rafters on a cold rainy day, feeling that if I let go I will fall—really fall. But I climb up, and for the next three and a half hours, I lay bead after bead. I put my helmet down, I strike an arc, and I see the welds. Four thirty, the buzzer rings. I slowly climb down. I'm tired, real tired. I don't want the guys to see how tired I am, but my legs hurt, my arms hurt. I walk slowly, my head down. I don't want to talk to anyone. I don't want to hear one more remark today. I just want to go home and take a hot bath. I gather my red toolbox, my lunch pail.

Randy says, "Don't think you're finished, Carlyle. We've got a good couple of weeks work up there." I can't wait to get these leather overalls off. I can't wait to soak in the tub.

Awards Night

§

Spring 1973. I park my yellow VW bus in the driveway. I come in the back door where I can peel off my overalls. Reuven is sitting in the front room, watching TV. He's staring. I yell, "What are you doing watching TV? You should be chopping wood—you know we don't have enough kindling. What's wrong with you?" I keep walking and peel off my clothes and jump into the hot bath–the clawed bathtub in the cold house.

Tears come down. I can't go back tomorrow. I have two more weeks of this. I'm going to scream. Reuven comes in. "What do you want?" I scream, "Can't I have some peace?"

He says, "I just want to tell you that I made Boys' Club, and we're having an Awards Night."

"Sure," I say. "Just leave me."

He walks out, head down. I crawl into bed.

I hear the television, louder than usual. I can't sleep. I crawl out of bed. Make some fried chicken from the freezer. I tell Reuven to come and eat something. He doesn't answer. I yell, "Don't forget to do your homework!"

I finish eating and crawl back into bed. Finally Reuven comes out and starts eating by himself. I yell, "Don't make a mess. Good night."

I can't sleep. My legs hurt. My eyes hurt. The house is cold, but I know I'll get up at six o'clock tomorrow, make my lunch, and drive down to the end of Harris Avenue and start my day over—I'll climb up the ladder, and I'll weld again, holding on, knowing that if I let go I'll fall.

Reuven keeps talking about Awards Night. Every night when I come home, I hear about it. The Boys' Club manager has a new system. He's giving the kids points for staying late after school to work on projects. Reuven rides his bike home afterwards. Some nights, he comes home later than me. I don't like it. He shouldn't be riding his bike through town at that time of the night.

I need to talk to this Boys' Club manager. I go to the building where the Boys' Club meets and storm into the middle of the room while Reuven is there with his friends.

"What are you doing here?" he says.

I ignore him and walk right over to the quiet, well-groomed young man who is showing a couple of boys how to build birdhouses. "Who do you think you are making these kids stay here so late?"

"Are you someone's mother?" he asks politely.

"Look," I tell him, "Reuven can't stay here this late. He shouldn't be riding his bike at this hour, and I can't pick him up like the other mothers do."

I stomp out. After that Reuven comes home early every night. He says the manager makes him leave early because of what I said. Somehow, he manages to earn enough points anyway.

The week before Awards Night, Reuven starts to get excited again. "Are you going to come and see me get my award?"

"We'll see," I tell him. But I know it won't work. No way. I can't go there and hang out with the other parents.

The week at the shipyard is crazy. I'm exhausted every night when I get home. On Friday, Reuven is waiting for me at the front door. "It's Awards Night. Did you remember?"

I collapse on the bed. "You'll have to find another way to get there," I tell him. He calls a friend and gets a ride and leaves without me.

CONVERSATIONS IN THE LUNCHROOM

ℰ

Spring 1974. The steam whistle shrieks at 11:00 a.m. Guys come out of sheds, down from ladders, out from behind machines. They file to the lunchroom, joking and laughing with each other, but not with me. The lunchroom is a small, sparse room. Windows along one side, cement floor, gray walls. In the center, a handful of wooden tables are pushed together, making one long, rectangular table. There are plain wooden benches around it. I find a place to sit and eat my salad.

"You're never going to make it here eating rabbit food," calls out Sam, a local who's worked here for years. In his two thick hands, he holds a large roast beef sandwich on homemade bread. "Want to work like a man, you've got to eat like a man." A few guys chuckle. Not friendly. Somebody makes a joke about vegetarians.

I look at the nude posters all around the lunchroom—women's bodies, all kinds of body parts. They're really bothering me now that I'm president of the local chapter of NOW (National Organization of Women). I'm working on women's equality. I'm working on women not being treated as sex objects. I get mad. "Hey, that's not fair. Take them down."

There's no answer. No one looks at me.

Then Fordy starts. "Okay, Carlyle, see here. It's your commie friends that're causing all the trouble. We should kill 'em all. It's your commie friends that got us into this mess."

"Hey," says Ted, "leave her alone."

"Okay, but she's always bitching. Nothing wrong with these posters. Hell, I gotta look at something. My ole lady ain't nothing to look at." Laughter.

Sam joins in. "It's her friends that got us into this mess anyway. Protesting the war. I'm sick of these protesters. What do they know? Our boys are dying over there, and all she knows is frickin' protests. I'm sick of it—that Bob Dylan guy, those Beatles. I don't want to hear any more. My cousin, Larry, came back with his legs shot off, and they're out there protesting. Why, just passing the college on the way home, I see them marching with their signs. Shit, Carlyle, you guys are nuts."

I eat my lunch, my usual salad in a plastic container. I hear him. I don't hear him. I don't want to hear him, and I don't want those posters up there. That I know. The buzzer rings, and we go back to work. I've had it. I can't stand looking at those posters of nude women at lunchtime any more.

I get home and call up a NOW friend in Seattle. "Hey," she says, "you can't let that happen. Strike back. Get a calendar of nude men and put them up."

I sneak into the lunchroom before work and put up my posters—nude men with thick arms, thick legs, posing. The buzzer rings for lunch. We all file in, one after another. Not a word. You can hear the wax paper crumbling, the lunch boxes opening. I sit there. No one says a word to me the whole half hour. No one talks the whole time.

The buzzer rings. We leave in silence. The next morning the female nude photos are back up when I file in for lunch. Randy, my boss says, "Carlyle, don't say a word. That's it. These women are staying with us." I open my plastic container and eat my salad in silence.

THE GUYS

&

In the time that I've been here, I've watched a ship being built from the ground up—and spent months inside its skeleton, welding steel sheets together.

One day, I'm at my station working on an overhead weld. Across the yard, I see a guy rolling an oxyacetylene tank. Not carrying it, rolling it. Why didn't I think of that? For two years, I've had to ask Pete, Fordy, Mike, or whoever else was around for help. No one ever told me to just roll it. Why couldn't someone have told me? It sure would have made it a lot easier.

Two guys walk past my workstation.

"Hey, Tom," one says, "what'd you do Saturday night—stop by this loose lady's place for a quick screw?"

"You kidding? I wouldn't screw her with your dick."

I'm home one Saturday night, and my boss, Randy, crawls into my house through a window. Wobbly and reeking of booze, he says he wants to fuck me. I throw a pitcher of water on him and tell him to get out.

One day, I'm strapped into a leather harness and dangled from a crane, way up in the sky, to weld a beam. "Hey, Carlyle," Dan, the union rep, shouts from below, "how 'bout giving me a little pussy tonight?"

Dan again, this time in the lunchroom. "I'm up for some serious action tonight. What time should I drop by?" Guys laugh. He does this every time we're in the lunchroom together. I used to get embarrassed. Now I'm just mad.

"Come at eight," I say, looking him right in the eye. "You drop by and show me what you got. I mean it."

"Wooooo!" the guys say. They laugh and hoot. "You lucky dog, Dan."

Dan is smiling, but it's an uneasy smile. He can see I'm serious. He fidgets and tries to laugh it off, as if it were all a big joke.

But I'm dead serious, and he knows it. I'll sleep with him just to shut him up.

I don't have to. He never shows up. He never bothers me again either. Oh, why didn't I think of this at the beginning? Why?

Happy Valley

&

I want to buy a cottage on Twenty-second Street. Fifteen thousand dollars. I call my father from the pay phone on the corner of Harris and Twenty-first Street. The seller is with me—I know him. He's a respected professor at Western Washington University. I put him on the phone, and my father starts interrogating him. I hear bits of his conversation.

The professor answers each question softly, with patience. I'm ready to scream. The professor hands me the phone. "Make sure he's not cheating you," I hear. "Make sure you get the right papers. Make sure it's not too much money—it seems way too much money to me."

"Okay, Okay." I make faces. My stomach makes noises. I hang up.

"What did he say?" I ask.

"I told him I would carry the note. I told him I wasn't cheating you. I told him you needed a house for you and Reuven. I don't think he believed me."

Why does my father always think I'm getting cheated? Why does he always worry about spending money? It seems like I'm always asking him for money. He always objects, but he always sends money when I really need it.

I think about how his life must have been. I've heard the stories about what it was like for immigrants coming to Ellis Island with nothing but the clothes on their backs. I've heard about the hard life in the shetl, having one pair of shoes and putting cardboard in them to keep out the cold.

Later when Reuven comes home from school, he asks if we're going to get the house. I tell him that my father complained but agreed to send the down payment.

BASEBALL

❧

Summer 1974. Reuven, like other nine-year-olds, wants to play softball, wants to be in the league.

Me. I come home so tired, soaking my body, trying to get rid of the toxins in my body.

The games. Watching games is part of the ritual—mothers cheering, mothers bringing goodies, mothers chatting with each other, comparing brownie recipes, telling stories about their kids. Mothers in Bellingham with polyester outfits, crosses around their necks, small diamond rings on their fingers, and teased hair.

Cheering, "Yea, Johnny! Yea, team, go, go!"

I can't face them.

I tell Reuven I won't go. I'm not like those mothers. I can't sit there alone. No one talks to me. Alone. Not part of the crowd, the mothers cheering for their sons.

I don't have a husband who works.

I don't have a husband I go home to and cook dinner for.

I don't have a husband to take care of.

I can't face them.

I can't face being different with my salt and pepper hair hanging down, with my tired legs wanting to buckle under.

I can't face it.

No, Reuven, I won't go.

I won't watch you play ball.

"But all the moms go."

"Well, they don't work," I say.

"But I want you to."

"No, I won't go. I don't have the time. I've got to be up early tomorrow for work."

He goes to the games.

He plays.

He doesn't have anyone to cheer for him.

Into the Bow

ℬ

"Carlyle, go down into the bow," Leonard tells me. "It'll keep you out of trouble."

"The bow?" I've heard Jimmy complain it's a tight spot.

"Yeah, the bow. We need to seal up the boat. Only you and Jimmy can fit."

I gather my torch, chipping hammer, 1017 rods, and wire lamp for when I get in there. I climb into the boat and walk across to the corner. I lower myself down the steel ladder, one rung at a time. I peek in. Pitch black. "All right," I say to myself. "Jimmy does it. You can do it."

It's a tight black space. I inch along, moving at an angle as my shoulders touch the wall. It's stuffy in here. It's dark in here, but I keep moving. I come to an even smaller space. I realize I have to crouch down, I realize I have to lie on my stomach and just inch along. "Oh boy," I think. "Leonard can't say I'm not earning my money today. In fact, we should get extra for this." It's not a long way, but the darkness crawls through with me. I stop for a minute to breathe. I smell soot. I give a little cough. The tightness of the space is a womb about to explode.

I crouch down, put a rod in the holder, put my helmet on, flip down the hood, and strike an arc. Fire comes through, light comes through, the white-hot intensity comes through. I weld bead after bead, crouching low. I'm buzzing with the sound of the electricity in this space. It's overhead welding and vertical. I have to hold my hand in place with the other hand. Weld after weld, molten pool after molten pool. I realize I can't stop for a break, come up for air. It would take too long, it would hurt too much to crawl out and back again, so I keep on welding. I keep on finishing a rod, putting up my helmet in the dark, and starting over again. Crouching in a corner in the dark. Crouching inside, holding the torch and making a bead across the metal plate— another part of me returns, the part of me that crawled underground.

I hear the whistle blow—the lunch whistle. I put down my torch and again inch my way out of the dark underground. When I come out, I hear Leonard say to Jimmy, "Go down and see how her overhead looks." Why is Leonard checking up on me? He knows I can do it. Jimmy comes out. He says something to Leonard I can't hear over the whirr of the crane. Leonard comes over to me, "Not bad, Carlyle, not bad. Okay, go back and finish up after lunch."

Fire at Fairhaven Shipyard

꒜

Randy and Leonard are walking around with the plans for the *Provider*. This side has to go up. They look at the plans again, point in another direction and talk some more. The buzzer rings at four thirty, and we continue to work. The buzzer rings at six thirty, and the day is over. My feet hurt. The next day and the next day after that. The pace is frenetic—we work long hours from 7:00 a.m. to 6:30 p.m. with half an hour for lunch and two fifteen-minute breaks.

The house goes up—the house where the controls of the boat are. It looks like a house sitting above the boat. Leads are all over the deck, and the big machine with lots of dials to control the settings is in the corner. I walk back and forth to adjust the machine to get the right setting. The guys don't walk as much—maybe not at all, but I walk. There's something about the pace, the leads all over, there's something not right. I can feel it. Leonard says the house has to be finished by Friday.

I can't handle the pace, the leads and other equipment all over, the plans lying around, the banging of metal, of wood. My stomach hurts. I'm sick—sick of this all. On Wednesday, I call in sick and stay in bed. On Thursday, I call in sick again. I live on the Southside. I hear sirens. I go outside my house. All day I've been rolled up in a ball in my house, but I'm outside now. The sirens. I know, I just know it's the shipyard. I look out, and the smoke is coming from Harris Avenue, and the sirens are moving toward Harris Avenue. I put on the radio, local news bulletin—fire at shipyard on Harris Avenue.

Pete comes by. "It's bad," he says. "The whole house is gone. All that work—there goes the deadline."

Friday is payday, and I go into the office. Leonard is sitting there with the paychecks. I look out, smell smoke, see charred ruins, see the boat without the house. I walk in, and Leonard says to me, "See what you've done." I was home when it happened, but it's my fault. Leonard tells me it's my fault, and on one level, I believe him. I take my check.

"Be here Monday," Leonard says. I get my helmet and walk up the plank to the boat. Randy is there surveying the damage.

"How ya feeling about this?" I ask him. I'm told that the fire started in my area, and Randy is the boss. Shame crawls all over me, and I wasn't even there.

"Hell," Randy says, "you could see this happening, the fire extinguishers didn't work, the leads all over. Hell, it's their fault."

Their fault! What is he talking about? It's my fault. I wasn't there, but somehow I feel it is my fault. Or if I were Randy, I would certainly feel it was my fault. But to blame it on the management? Wow! I realize right that moment that men think differently than women. Men don't think anything is their fault. I think everything is my fault.

I take my paycheck to the bank up Harris Avenue to cash it.

BOAT PEOPLE

ᚷ

Spring 1975. Some guys are building a catamaran–a boat to sail around the world, catch fish, and be independent. I get acquainted with one of the guys and meet the rest of them. They ask me to do some welding for them. "Sure," I say.

Reuven comes with me. He likes being there. They're out in the harbor on the south side. From a few pieces of steel, the boat begins to take shape.

Reuven starts to spend a lot of time with them—he's a mascot. He likes bringing them stuff. He spends nights there, afternoons, weekends.

During the week, he comes in the door just as I'm getting ready to leave for work. "What are you doing here?" I say. I know he slept over on the boat and has to go to school.

"Oh," he says, "I just wanted to check in."

So it becomes the routine. Most nights he sleeps on the boat with the boat people, stops by the house in the morning, and then goes to school and back to the boat after school. Many evenings I don't see him. Sometimes I go down to the boat and say, "Hi." Sometimes I just stay home and soak in the tub after a long day at the shipyard.

Provider Launch

ℬ

August 1975. "Everyone on board!" Leonard shouts as he strides across the yard toward the water. He sees me with welding rod in hand. "That means you, Carlyle. All hands on board."

We gather at the edge of the dock—Randy, Mark, Pete, Mike—all the people who've been working on the *Provider*. She's ready to be launched in Bellingham Bay. I know every inch of this 120-foot Alaska king crab boat. I had the honor of laying the first weld.

Someone lays out a plank, and one by one, we cross it to the deck. I've never been to a launching. Most of us haven't. We know what went into building the boat. For twenty months, we've crawled in and out and climbed up and down, welding rods in hand.

When we're all aboard, someone unties the thick rope. The boat vibrates. I stand at the very edge of the deck, pressed against the rail, and watch as we inch away from the dock.

The men are cheering. All the guys who haven't been nice to me, this day we ride together, this day we are in sync as we ride the waves, as we see this finished boat in all its glory, riding up and down, and we all hold on together seeing the fruit of many, many months of work. I've never seen the guys like this. I shout along with them, feeling part of them, but not part of them. Then people start hugging. Pete throws his arms around me and lifts me off the deck. Mike wraps his arms around us both and then everyone's together, the whole crew, in a single big group hug, laughing and shouting as the rain falls and the *Provider* rolls and chugs toward the open waters.

My Father Visits Bellingham

℘

My father calls me at the house I bought recently at 913 Mason Street. He says he'd like to come for a visit.

"A visit?" I say.

"Yeah, by myself, without your mother." My father has never traveled alone. "I want to see you and Reuven."

I pick him up at the Bellingham airport. He looks so out of place—a short man, an old man with a big jacket and a little bag. He's staying for the week. Reuven grabs his hand and walks with him to the car. We walk into the house on the hill. I just open the front door—no key, no lock.

"Don't you lock the door?" my father says.

"Oh, we don't need locks around here."

"Well, that's not a good idea. I'll look into it. Don't you have a key?"

"I think we had one once, but it got lost."

I show my father his room—room upstairs next to mine. It feels funny, my father without my mother in my funky house in Bellingham, sleeping in a room next to mine. But he's polite. He talks to me. He plays the stock market. Moments with my father, whom I really don't know.

The Fairhaven Tavern. I take him to our hangout one night. My friends are sitting around drinking beer—my welding friends.

"Hi, Joan," I hear.

"What's happening?"

I go around and introduce my father to the fishermen, the welders, the locals.

"This is my father, Morris Waldman."

"Cool," says one of the guys.

"Cool," becomes a chorus.

My father starts talking to the fishermen. I look up, and there's my father sitting on a stool, telling stories—stories about his grocery store, how he started it during the depression by borrowing ten dollars to use as a down payment for the store at an auction. The guys are enthralled. He starts giving advice about running a business. The fishermen, all self-employed, are all around him. He's high up on his stool—they don't want him to stop. "More. Tell us more," I hear. My father tells story after story about his life—poor immigrant boy making it, working hard.

When we leave, he's smiling, happy. Says he likes it here. Likes being without my mother. "Let's go back again," he says.

In the house, he pulls apart the groceries in the pantry and organizes it. Then he goes out and buys more groceries. He pulls apart books, papers, stuff, and organizes it, and when I come home from work one day, he's working on the front door. "What are you doing?" I say.

"You've got to have a lock—you can't leave it open like this. You're going to get robbed."

"Dad," I say, "no one gets robbed around here."

"Well, you need a lock," and every day for the week, he works on putting in the lock. He tells me my house isn't level, it's hard to get it in right.

"Dad, it's a hundred-year-old house—it's not going to be level."

"Well, I'll work on getting it to work."

He walks with Reuven. He helps Reuven with his paper route.

After Reuven is in bed one night, he talks to me. He tells me he never loved my mother. He thought he was marrying someone with culture because they had a picture hanging over the sofa, but he realized during the honeymoon that my mother was crazy and he didn't love her.

I'm stunned. I've never thought about my father having feelings, being vulnerable.

"Why didn't you leave?" I ask.

"Oh, you don't leave a marriage," he says back. "I wouldn't think of it."

I see my father as a vulnerable man who came to the United States and started working right away. He never had a chance to go to school. He was put in kindergarten at age thirteen, and when he got up from the little seat, he was stuck. All the kids laughed, and he never went back to school again. I see another side of him without my mother next to him. I don't feel threatened. I don't feel numb. I have a father.

When he leaves to go back home, he tries to hug me goodbye. I want to. I want to have a nice father, but I step back for a second. I try hugging him goodbye.

"Thanks, Dad."

"Oh, thank you," he says.

I turn when he tries to kiss me.

"We better get going," I say.

Reuven gives him a big hug. My father breaks down and cries.

"I'm sorry," he says. "I'm sorry."

I don't know what he's trying to say.

"Let's get to the airport," I say.

ROSES FOR MOTHER'S DAY

$\mathscr{E}$

Reuven and I are living on Mason Street in the old Victorian house with creaking fir floors, with no insulation, with stained glass windows. I come in exhausted every night, peel off my overalls, and get in the tub, the old fashioned claw-foot tub.

We have a round table in the front room where we eat, a round table that I got at Nasty Jack's in La Conner for fifty dollars. Nicked, scarred, but an oak round table.

Mother's Day. I come downstairs, and there are a dozen roses—red roses in a vase on the table. Reuven, blond hair, innocent eyes, is sitting at the table in his overalls.

"What's this?" I say.

"For Mother's Day," he says.

And then I say, "Where did you get this? Why did you get this? Where did you get the money? We don't have money like that to waste. We don't have money."

I look at the red roses. That's for rich people. I see my cousin Ralphie always buying, buying things he can't afford. Flashy—that's what my family said about him.

Reuven puts his head down. I continue screaming, "We can't afford it."

$\mathscr{E}$

Memories. I'm ten years old. I want to buy my mother a present, a special present for her birthday, November 18. There's a gift store on the avenue—Maple Avenue. My mother goes in there a lot. I go in and tell Mr. Bauman, the owner, I'm looking for a birthday present for my mother. He shows me a long table in the middle of the store with all kinds of gifts.

"Take your time," he says. I do. I finger each item, but I can't decide. I tell him I'll come back tomorrow.

Every day for two weeks I come back after school, and I look at all that Mr. Bauman has, on the table, on the shelves, and in the glass cabinet that has a lock and key. I want my present to be perfect. I want my mother to know that I care. I work hard to get the perfect present. But I can't decide. What should I choose?

On November 16, I say to myself, "I have to pick the right present." I do. A silver tray. A beautiful, shining silver tray.

I ask Mr. Bauman to wrap it carefully. I pay. I carefully walk home with the wrapped silver tray. I want it to be a surprise. I sneak into my room and put it under my clothes in the dresser.

On November 18 in the morning, I burst into my mother's room, so proud, and I hand her the wrapped silver tray. She opens it and puts it down, not saying anything.

"Don't you like it, Ma?" She turns away and screams, "It's not personal. I don't want another silver tray to clean."

The next day she returns the silver tray and buys herself a cameo broach with a blue background. Through the years she says, "What's wrong with you—you never buy me a birthday present or send me a Mother's Day card."

LAST DAYS OF WELDING

℘

Spring 1977. The steam whistle blows. We file into the lunchroom, the small steel Quonset hut next to the administration building. Pete and Mike and Tim have all left the shipyard. Yesterday, I was out sick. Today I walk in for lunch. I take out my plastic container and start munching my usual salad. The guys open up their steel black or blue lunch boxes and take out their big sandwiches with thick home-made bread.

Bob, my new boss—Crew Cut Bob we call him—sits across from me. He's quiet. So different from Randy, who laughed and his belly shook, who used to yell across the ship, "Hey, Carlyle, don't be so lazy. Get me a monkey wrench out of the bin." Bob is not only quiet; he also speaks softly. He stands straight, looks straight ahead. He keeps to himself. Bob is a devout churchgoer from Lynden. I've seen his mouth curve upward for a smile, but certainly no hearty belly laugh, no curse words flying through the air.

The jackhammers are going outside. The claw hammers are pounding, Dan starts shouting above the drilling, "So, Carlyle, where were you yesterday? Bob here was out. You were out."

"Yeah," chimes in Fordy. "What were you two doing? Now, come on, tell us what ya two were doing all day. Tell us. Ya have a good time together?"

Then Tom, "Yeah, ya probably planned this for weeks—right Carlyle? Tell us about it, Carlyle. What ya doing bothering our poor boss here—couldn't leave him alone. Right. Look, he never bothers anybody, and ya had to have some. Picking on poor Bob. That'll teach you to be out during the week."

Bob's eyes are down. Bob's cheeks are red, beet red against fair skin, red against his blue coveralls. I look at him. He doesn't look at me. Bob doesn't say anything. Please, Bob, say something. I want to throw up. I want to run.

I start, "I've been sick."

"Oh, yeah, I bet," says Dan in the background. "Carlyle, you can't fool us, got it? We know you two were romping together, probably out in some field."

The whistle blows; lunch boxes close. I get up. I hear, "Don't try that again, Carlyle." I walk over to Bob. He turns and walks the other way. His face is still red. I need my afternoon welding assignment. When we get to the ship, I walk toward him. He sees me and walks the other way. I want to crawl under the ship.

Bob gives Fordy and Jack instructions. Fordy walks towards me and says, "You're to go up top." I put my chipping hammer on my belt, pick up my helmet, grab some rods from the cabinet and walk across to the ship and climb up. I put a rod in the holder, put my helmet on, flip down the hood, and strike an arc. Fire comes through, light comes through, the white hot intensity comes through. I weld bead after bead. Tears come to my eyes.

What am I doing? I can't stand this anymore. I want to die. I can't stand it. All of it. Dan screaming at me when I'm hanging on up top, "Hey, Carlyle, how about some pussy tonight?" The lunchroom, the female nude posters I have to stare at. Joke after joke, sex talk after sex talk. I finish the rod. I flip up my helmet, put in another rod and continue. More light shines through, more molten metal. The pieces come together. Power holding the rod. Making fire. My hand moves. I just want to feel the torch in my hand, my hood going down, the fire, the burning. I can feel it.

I've got this torch now. I'm making fire. I'm putting things together. I'm alive in the shipyard. I'm home now. I'm thirty-six. I've been living in this underground my whole life. What's going to happen to me, to Reuven? I say the words don't matter to me, but they do. I'm wearing my long dangling bead earrings, the only sign I am a woman in this world as the words split me open. I can't listen anymore. I can't hear one more time, "Lady, go home. You don't belong here." I've got to come up for air.

ENOUGH

&

It takes a few more days. I show up for work. I go through the motions. I'm not expecting to do what comes next, but in an instinctive moment before lunch I take my chipping hammer, the rod, and my torch. I walk across the yard—the yard with boats in dry-dock, the yard overlooking Bellingham Bay, the yard I know so well. The guys are at their stations.

I stomp across and throw down the torch, throw down the rods, the chipping hammer. I hold tight to my helmet, and I scream with all my might. I hear echoes in my ears, but I don't stop. I won't stop. I scream, "I quit! I'm finished! Hear me, all of you? I quit!"

Fordy and Jim pick up their helmets and stare. Others stare. I don't care. No one stops me. No one can stop me now. I don't ever want to see this place again. I don't ever want to crawl through the wires of the ship hearing, "Hey, Carlyle, how about some pussy tonight?" I don't ever want to hear the banging of the chipping hammers, feel the hot sparks go down between my breasts, screaming and wiggling with Fordy and Dan laughing.

I don't know what's going to happen. I don't know how I'm going to feed us, but I won't do it, hear me, I won't! I walk straight. I walk with my head up high. I know now that I am free. I don't have to live like this. I am a journeyman welder. I've worked for years to get the right to weld. And I did it. I welded flat, vertical, and overhead.

My body is broken, my heart is broken, but I am not broken. I know I can raise the torch, and I can say I did it. I remember Haight-Ashbury. I remember Ned saying, "Hang on. Someday it will be different." I have a child. I have a home. I'll get another job. I thought it would be different. I've learned how to use a come-along, a pad-eye. I've learned how to spend hours looking up, welding overhead. I will find a way, launch in another direction. I'm raw right now, but I get in my yellow VW bus and drive up Harris Avenue. I don't stop until I get home, take off my leathers, take a hot bath, and let the feelings wash over me. I wait for Reuven to come home from school.

PART 6

§

LOOKING FORWARD

THE NEXT GENERATION

ଔ

Bellingham, Washington, 1980. Reuven is fourteen years old, almost a young man. I can feel the split. How can I have a man in the house? A man with hormones, testosterone, a young man. He needs to get out of the house.

I know Mary Kay Becker, a state legislator. She's told me about a two-week program for freshman high school students to work in the legislature as pages. "Sure," Mary Kay says, "send him down."

Two weeks, Reuven sees how the legislature works, two weeks he's there as a page. When I pick him up in the state capital, Olympia, he says, "I want to go back." He's had a taste of a world away from me and my crazies.

ଔ

Summertime. I'm invited to a party on the hill for Senator Magnuson who is seeking re-election. Reuven comes with me. I don't want to stay, though. Reuven follows me down the block to a friend's house. A few minutes later, he says he wants to go back to the party.

"Sure."

When I go back to pick Reuven up, he's sitting on a footstool, talking intently to the senator and his wife. From where I'm standing, I overhear a few words of their conversation.

I know he's trying to sell the senator on the idea of making him a page.

"Oh, I have someone this year," says the senator, "but you can apply for next year." We get the forms, and Reuven fills them out.

❦

It's Thursday night. I'm working in Seattle making granola— pounds and pounds of granola. I still live in Bellingham, but I stay in Seattle during the week. I get a call at work. It's Reuven. "The page got homesick," he says.

"What?" I say.

"They want me," he says. "I gotta go. I want to go to Washington. I need to be there by Sunday."

Featherstone Reid, Senator Magnuson's aide (who is called Feather), repeats the story to me. He says, "We have a huge stack of applications, but the senator keeps saying, 'I want that kid from Bellingham.'" Senator Magnuson doesn't know that Reuven has just turned fifteen.

I put Reuven on a red-eye to DC. I put a fifteen-year-old on a plane to a new life, away from me, away from Bellingham. He calls me Monday night after his first day on the floor. "Ted Kennedy brushed past me. Can you believe it? Ted Kennedy!" Feather takes Reuven to buy a suit. Feather sets him up in his apartment on the couch.

After brushing past Senator Kennedy, Reuven decides to walk into the senator's office. He meets Melody Miller, Senator Kennedy's deputy press secretary, who has been with the Kennedys since JFK was in office. She takes a liking to Reuven. She shows him around. She introduces him to senators, to chiefs of staff, to aides. She opens up the tunnels of the underground world there.

Three months later, Magnuson loses his election. Reagan becomes president. Reuven doesn't want to come home, but Magnuson isn't a senator anymore. Reuven follows Senator Scoop Jackson through the halls, through the underground tunnels.

"No, Reuven," Senator Jackson says. "I don't want a page. They're too much trouble."

A few days later Reuven calls me. He's staying in Washington. He's going to work for Senator Jackson.

Epilogue

ℬ

Seattle, Washington, 2011. I look out the window from my apartment on Queen Anne Hill. Lights—the Space Needle, Big Howe Park, the city in lights. Reuven's just come in carrying Nava, my youngest granddaughter, for her first sleepover. She's four. Yes, she wants a sleepover away from the busy home with Adi, Liat, Zev, Wendy, and Reuven. Just us. Reuven blows up the air mattress next to my bed and kisses her good-bye.

She changes into her PJs and pull-up and brushes her teeth. This is how it goes. We lie in her bed—the blowup bed. I read a story, *I Like Me*, then another, *No, David*. "Okay, Nava, it's late." She puts her head down. I go into my bed next to her, put my head down. I hear, "I'm hungry."

"What do you want?" She follows me to the kitchen.

"Cereal."

I get the cereals down.

"Oh, the colored circles."

"I'm almost out," I say. "But we have enough."

"Okay."

She finishes the cereal; I finish my yogurt and frozen berries.

She goes back to the blowup bed. I go back to my bed. I hear, "I want to be with you."

"Sure, Nava, come in my bed."

I hear, "I'm not tired."

"Just lie down," I say.

"I'm still hungry."

We go out to the kitchen again. I give her a cup of chocolate milk with her favorite straw, and we go back to my bedroom.

"I want to sleep in my bed."

"Fine."

She lies down.

"It's too dark in here."

I get up and put the bathroom light on.

"It's still too dark."

Then I put the kitchen light softly on. I come back, and she's asleep, eyes closed.

I'm seventy years old now. I never dreamed I would live this long. I never dreamed that I would have the life I have now. Grandkids. Walk. Write. Twelve-step programs. Just being.

I look back at the pattern of my life's journey—from the Jewish immigrant neighborhood of my childhood, through mental institutions, the Haight-Ashbury of the sixties, and Fairhaven Shipyard—to now.

The thread:

Looking back.

Looking back now.

The moments.

The moment at Dammash. I have to get sane. There's always been a voice in me, a small insistent voice that knew the way. I didn't know I had that voice. I didn't know until I wrote this memoir. This voice that carried me through. This voice that, when all the other words were crowding my mind—my mother's voice, "You're fat, you're stupid"—this small stubborn voice defied all the conventions of the time. This little voice pulled me through the sanity hearing at Dammash.

This voice, the first night home, holding the baby close to me, not knowing if he would live or not, watching the night slowly tick by, seeing the light and knowing we would make it. I didn't know how, but I knew, and this voice put me on a path, not the path of my child-hood expectations, not the path of my parents, but a path of letting people in, letting people care for me when I couldn't. Ned with his wisdom—"Hold on. Someday it will be different." Ned, in the most unexpected ways, allowing me to follow my intuition, helping me to keep Reuven, making sure he was cared for, supporting me in learning to become a welder instead of following a more traditional career path. On an outer level, it didn't make sense, but on an inner level, it was my journey, my way to get myself out of the basement—holding the torch, feeling the power. It's taken a lifetime. It's taken years of therapy and spiritual practice; it's taken years of working with my body, my memories steeped in my body.

Renee Pat opened me, started me on the journey, allowed me to separate from my parents, to begin to find my way. Ned gave me the framework, the tools. Subud, my spiritual practice, helped me connect with the energy in my body and with the world outside myself, providing a deeper way of being. Hadiyah is the name I adopted after joining Subud. So many others, network chiropractor Dr. David Breitbach and yoga teacher Michael Suzerris—all working with the body, the memories stored in my cells. Touch me and I would scream with the memories, but slowly, by releasing the trauma, though it didn't go away, it found a place in my being, a place so that I have room—to hold Nava's hand, to get Zev a water bottle holder for his bike, to watch Liat at her gymnastic tournaments, to stand on the bimah with Adi, my eldest grandaughter at her Bat Mitsvah. I didn't have a Bat Mitzvah. Jewish girls in my town, at my synagogue, in the fifties, weren't allowed a Bat Mitzvah. The individual ceremony was only for boys. I ran away from Judaism for most of my adult life. Now my son's children and his wife, Wendy, light the Shabbat candles. My grandkids get Bat and Bar Mitzvahs. I'm here. Watching. I'm here, the *savta*, the grandma. Maybe it takes a lifetime to understand one's path on this earth; maybe it takes a lifetime to feel the life force all around. Most of my life, I plodded from moment to moment, from one trauma to the next.

I haven't had what I thought I wanted—a conventional family, a partnership. Instead my adult life has been devoted to healing, listening to the small distinct voice inside me, letting her find her way, letting her survive on the outside and letting people in on the inside. There are many gifted healers out there. I let them into my life at different times at different junctures. Now, my writing practice, my writing groups sustain me.

I want to tell my story because I'm still here. I'm here holding my young granddaughter's hand. I'm here walking through the Olympic National Park, I'm here doing yoga almost every day. I'm here, not in the back wards, not doped up on medication. I'm here alive, letting the light in. For that I am grateful, and I want to give hope to others. As long as I'm alive, there is a life force in me, there's a life force in all of us. May the light shine.

Acknowledgments

§

After more than ten years on the path to telling this story, I have many teachers, many good supportive people to thank. Among them are:

Bob Ray and Jack Remick, through their year-long class at the University of Washington Extension and sessions at Lousia Café, gave me the passion and framework to keep putting my words on paper.

I met Matt Rizzo and Anne Herman in the class with Bob and Jack, and we've worked together regularly for over nine years to support one another's efforts in writing our memoirs. Matt has spent countless hours developing my writing pieces into stories.

In her workshops in New York and Taos, New Mexico, Natalie Goldberg gave me permission to start writing and provided the basic orientation that I have followed in writing this memoir.

The East Coast Loop is a group of writers who follow Natalie Goldberg's approach and work together online. I thank the members of the Loop for all their encouragement, good advice, and reading of the manuscript.

Craft, craft, craft. Priscilla Long has taught me the art of the sentence, the art of the paragraph through many classes, many exercises. Her teachings are available in her book, *The Writer's Portable Mentor: A Guide to Art, Craft, and the Writing Life,* and I've been lucky enough to be in her classes. Priscilla has been a true mentor, taking me from the very basics of writing to an understanding of the publishing process. Thank you, Priscilla.

Dorothy Randall Gray was one of my first teachers when I started writing back in the eighties in Brooklyn. With her dramatic teaching style and open heart, she pushed me to write from the gut. Through Dorothy, I was introduced to the International Women's Writing Guild (IWWG) and went to several summer workshops where I was encouraged to keep writing.

Sara Ann Friedman has been with me through it all, from my earliest attempts at writing in Brooklyn to the present, contributing her expertise and long hours to bringing refinement and structure to the work.

Over the forty years that I've known her, Esther Helfgott has given me much valuable assistance with her sharp eye, knowledge and love of literature, and insightful perspective.

I want to thank all my writing friends who so graciously read the manuscript and gave me support and critical feedback: Arleen Williams, Anita Landa, Peter Jackson, Cathy Leichteig, and others.

I'm grateful for my brother Paul, who has traveled the path with me, giving me practical support and serving as an anchor in my life.

And Julie Fretzin worked closely with me in the final stage of putting all the pieces together to give form, at last, to my memoir. This was especially meaningful because Julie and I were together in the Foundation in the sixties, and she knows my story firsthand. It wouldn't have happened without Julie's calm and respectful manner. Thank you.

About the Author

ß

Hadiyah Joan Carlyle is now old enough to be a part of history. In the sixties, she was a single parent in Haight-Ashbury, San Francisco. In the seventies, she was the first and only female shipyard welder in Bellingham, Washington, north of Seattle. She completed the certificate program in Memoir Writing through the University of Washington Extension. Her poems and essay have been published in *Shine the Light: Sexual Abuse and Healing in the Jewish Community* by Rachel Lev and *Escaping the Yellow Wallpaper* by Elayne Clift.